THE INN CHEF

Creative Ingredients,
Sensational Flavors

Michael Smith

Callawind
Publications Inc.

Montreal

The Inn Chef: Creative Ingredients, Sensational Flavors

Copyright © 1999 by Callawind Publications Inc.
Select excerpts reprinted from *Open Kitchen: A Chef's Day at The Inn at Bay Fortune* by Michael Smith © 1998 by Callawind Publications Inc.

CATALOGUING IN PUBLICATION DATA
Smith, Michael, 1966–
     The Inn chef : creative ingredients, sensational flavors

Includes index.
Companion cookbook to the television series The Inn chef.
ISBN 1-896511-14-7

     1. Cookery.   1. Title.

TX715.6.S5828 1999   641.5'09717'7   C99-901054-9

Book design by Shari Blaukopf. Copy editing by Shaun Oakey. Indexing by Christine Jacobs.

10 9 8 7 6 5 4 3 2 1

Printed in Canada.
Product/brand names are trademarks or registered trademarks of their respective trademark holders.
Tabasco® is a registered trademark exclusively of McIlhenny Co., Avery Island, LA 70513.

Callawind Publications Inc. (www.callawind.com)
     1000-20 St-Jean Boulevard, Suite 536, Pointe Claire, Quebec, Canada H9R 5P1
     2083 Hempstead Turnpike, PMB 355, East Meadow, New York, USA 11554-1711

Distributed in North America by Firefly Books Ltd. (www.fireflybooks.com)
     3680 Victoria Park Avenue, Willowdale, Ontario, Canada M2H 3K1

The Inn Chef television series is produced by Inn Chef Productions Ltd. (www.innchef.com)
     1657 Barrington Street, Suite 404, Halifax, Nova Scotia, Canada B3J 2A1

Acknowledgments

◇

This tale is dedicated to all who help conceive, develop, produce, and broadcast *The Inn Chef* and to all the artists who have taught and learned with me in the kitchens of my career.

I am thankful to the farmers, fishermen, and other guests for sharing their living art with all of us and to Team Cuisine for strutting their stuff on screen. It's not always easy on our side of the lens!

In particular I am grateful to my production teams, who have embraced the creation of the show and this book as fervently as I. Our collective efforts define *The Inn Chef*.

And as for all of you on the other side of the lens: thanks for watching! I am humbled by the opportunity to share my passion for cuisine and life with you. I hope you have as much fun watching as we have making the show!

Contents

◇

MAIN COURSES

From the Sea

From the Land

A TIME for CHOCOLATE
COCONUT CLOCK TOWER
with PINEAPPLE VANILLA
SAUCE and the CORRECT
TIME . . .

Introduction

The most preposterous idea I ever had was to create a cooking show!

Usually — all bias aside! — my ideas are great. Sometimes they're flops. "Sure, Michael," everybody said, "a cooking show's a great idea!" They sounded the same way when I said I wanted to bury a stuffed lamb in the ground for 12 hours. Well, the lamb was a hit, so why shouldn't a TV show be a hit too?

Sometimes the nuttiest ideas are the best, and *The Inn Chef* has certainly proved the point. Initially I saw the show as furthering the ideals of my kitchen, as a means to share our energy and passion with more than just the guests in the dining room. I have always been proud of my untraditional approach to kitchen management, one that empowers the individual and disregards the autocratic hierarchy of the past. To me cuisine is only improved by taking it from the proverbial pedestal to a place where all can enjoy and appreciate it, free of the all-too-typical pretensions that often weigh it down. All of this energy inspired my approach to the show, and I am happy to report that my original goals have been achieved.

Television is a unique way to communicate. By trading off the detail of time and place for the bright, broad brushstrokes of the moment, a show is able to reach a vast audience. What may be lost in the translation is more than compensated for by the inspiration of the message, and by the viewers' confidence that they are part of the dynamic. The inherent challenge to the performer, or in my case the cook, is to know where to generalize and summarize and where to be specific and direct. Above all, the message must entertain. These are not lessons learned in even the best chefs' school!

I am grateful to share the joy and passion that have defined my cooking since my mom and I made cookies together. I am humbled by the responsibility of the medium, to be accurate and articulate. I am amazed at the effect a word or glance in front of a camera can have. I am honored by all of the people who have told me how much they enjoyed recreating one of my recipes. And of course I am thrilled to represent chefs everywhere and show that we have the best careers on the planet.

Through the show, I have met many extraordinary people. I have learned new skills and traveled to new places. Our show has struck a chord with viewers everywhere who enjoy our own blend of kitchen action and creative cuisine. I have enjoyed every moment and am proud of the influence *The Inn Chef* has had on cuisine everywhere. This book is my attempt to distill the people, places, and energy of the show. I hope you enjoy it. Now let's get cooking!

Welcome to
The Inn Chef's Kitchen

◇

As a prominent chef one of my greatest challenges is to convince my students, staff, and viewers that they can and do create cuisine the same way I do.

One of the inherent risks in becoming good at something and wanting to share it is the intimidation you may inspire. Cooks who tell me that they can't hope to match what I do, that I have some mysterious ability granted only to a fortunate few, often frustrate me. The only mystery to me is how so many mediocre cooks end up as the chef of pretentious restaurants while brilliant home cooks go unheralded. As elaborate, risky, or complicated as my food may seem at first glance or taste, it's actually as simple as I can possibly make it. In fact, I imagine that you and I are doing the same thing, the only difference being our level of experience and training. The following three guides are the basis to everything I do in my kitchen; indeed, as food often seems to be, they are a metaphor for life in general.

Use great ingredients

Ingredients are the raw material of the art form, the paint on the brush, the unchiseled rock. Everything in cuisine begins with the purity and goodness of awesome ingredients. That may seem obvious, but don't take it for granted. If you put the time and effort into stocking your kitchen with the finest possible ingredients, magic will result. You will gain an appreciation for the seasons and the rich rewards to be found in your own backyard. You will understand why as a chef half of my time is spent driving back roads, shaking hands, and leaping with joy at the discovery of a new heirloom apple tree or a fisherman who will bring me back sea urchins. This is the first step for a very good reason: cuisine celebrates the purity of its ingredients. In my kitchen the ingredients come before the recipe. A trip to the farmers' market is always a prelude to inspiration, a way to fan the spark of culinary creation that defines my cooking. Look beyond the surface; learn to understand and appreciate the nuances that define each of the multitude of onion varieties and why a plum tomato makes better sauce than its kin. Don't assume that just because the label says "olive oil" that you are any better off than if you had first cold pressing canola oil. There is a reason why strawberry shortcake in January doesn't taste right!

Cook with simplicity and respect

Our role as cooks in the creation of cuisine is insignificant compared to mother nature's. She defines 90 percent of my cooking because I strive not to overshadow her efforts. Why go through all the effort to find the most amazing vine-ripened sun-warmed hand-picked tomato only to obscure its inherent goodness with four vegetables, five herbs, two spices, and cheap wine? Such recipes exist, but they ignore the reality of cuisine that inspires me to highlight the beauty of my ingredients. I strive to accent them, to polish them, to give them a stage from which to shout, "Hey! I'm the best damn tomato you will ever taste!" I believe a recipe should celebrate the characteristics of its primary ingredients by just nudging them toward my flavor goals. Avoid overblown techniques that simmer away all pretense of freshness before puréeing any remaining form. Strive to showcase the purity of the ingredient's form, leaving your guests in awe of your remarkable cooking ability. (You don't have to point out that old man Jones down the road was really responsible for the flavor of the tomatoes.) I am honestly inspired by the diversity and quality of the bounty available to me.

Share the results

This is perhaps where home cooks have the lead. In my experience there can be far too much mechanical emphasis in professional cooking to allow for the pure satisfaction of a guest enjoying your efforts. The best chefs understand this dynamic and encourage young cooks to celebrate the process and not to lose touch with the overall goal of satisfying their guests. At home this energy seems effortless — why else would you spend all day in the kitchen for a few fleeting moments of culinary fame? It is for this very reason that I have done so well as a chef and ultimately as the star of my own cooking show: I am sharing. Cuisine is so amazingly life-affirming that I can't help but want to show it off, to celebrate the limitless expression of the art, and tell a few stories along the way!

So you see, we are not all that different, we professional culinarians. Unlike home cooks, we may be required to put in longer hours and be able to spout obscure culinary theory, but at heart we are all just cooks, filling our baskets, lighting our fires, and inviting our friends over. Cheers!

Behind the scenes
on the Set of *The Inn Chef*

◈

Lights, camera, action, and cut . . . It takes months of effort on the part of a very dedicated team to make just one episode of *The Inn Chef* a reality.

veryone who is part of the process contributes to the creative energy that defines the show you see. Although I hog the screen time, here is the cast of thousands on both sides of the camera that makes it happen:

Team Cuisine Jennifer Healey, Craig Stelmack, and Craig Flinn: These are the folks who are very busy when the camera's not rolling trying to get ready to look very busy when the camera is rolling. They test the recipes and set up for them, sometimes three times if I blow a take!

Co-Producers Gretha Rose and Johanna Eliot: The producers run the production company that makes the show. They stay up late at night wondering whether everything will fall into place and make sure in the morning that everything does. By afternoon there's always something else to worry about.

Creative Producer Michael MacDonald: The Boss! Michael essentially oversees all aspects of the production, from writing and planning to shooting and editing. He calls the shots and has the vision of what should and

sometimes does happen. It may be my kitchen and my recipes, but it's his set, and what he says goes.

Director Theresa Séguin: The other Boss! Theresa runs the show while we are on location shooting the stories. She deals with the reality of location shooting where anything that can go wrong waits until the cameras are rolling!

Assistant Director James Nicholson: Every kitchen has a sous-chef that really gets the job done while the chef is off dreaming. The AD plays that role in our make-believe kitchen. He's the guy who organizes everything and generally makes sure that we're on track and in focus and that the cameras are turned on when they're supposed to be.

Unit Manager Shawn MacDonald: Shawn gets everyone to the right place at the right time and facilitates the behind-the-scenes details that make the shoot flow as smoothly as it does. Shawn is also our location scout when we hit the road to shoot various segments. He travels to each site and scopes it out looking for surprises to hide before we arrive! He also helps me with all the research it takes to make the show.

Director of Photography Dean Brousseau: Dean makes sure that the set is lit properly so I always look bright eyed and fresh — even after many hours of filming! When we are rolling he operates the close-up camera that focuses on the insides of the pots and my lightning-fast onion chopping. He also sets up the amazing shots of the finished plates that start and finish each show.

Cameraman Patrick Doyle: The rock and roll guy. Pat operates the mobile camera that makes up many of the shots shown. He has to be very smooth and is a wizard at getting the shot. He's also the guy who won't turn off his camera when I make a mistake, hence the blooper segment at the end of each show!

Audio Recordist Kate Kechnie: It's not easy making me sound good by hiding microphones all over the place. Kate makes it happen, though. She is a true connoisseur of sound and works magic with her gear.

Key Grip Corey Bulger: Hustle is Corey's middle name. He has one speed — fast — and needs it. Corey is the guy who sets up the gear, hangs the lights, finds missing things, and generally keeps everybody else supplied with paddles for our collective canoe ride. He also helps set up for the plate shots at the beginning and end of the show. His right-hand man, Rob Turner, picks up everything that Corey knocks over!

Editors Peter Giffen, Jim Patriquin, and Jeff Fish: The real wizards. These guys take hours and hours of footage and turn it into 30 minutes of fast-paced, logical action — a technically demanding job that requires great skill. They also come up with all the fun special effects on the show. Their assistant, John Feron, makes sure that everybody is plugged in and full of coffee.

Catering Chef Jeff McCourt: Nothing can get done without Jeff! He takes time out from his busy schedule as the chef at The Inn at Bay Fortune, where we film, to cook for the production crew. He even serves as culinary adviser to me when my ideas get a bit too wacky.

And last but not least, producers' assistants Rita De Nicola and Angela Campbell: Guess who the real power behind the throne is? These ladies rock!

A day on the set is fast-paced and fun. At any moment disaster or triumph can strike. Everyone is having a good time and we feed off of each other's energy, so it's hard to have a bad day. There's a lot of kidding around, but when the director yells "Lock 'em up," we jump and assume our roles. Most of the crew are seasoned professionals and have seen it all in the film business, but they are always amazed at the live cuisine that they are part of.

We film on-location at The Inn at Bay Fortune on Prince Edward Island, where I designed a state-of-the-art kitchen that we now use for the show. It has special high ceilings for all the filming gear and is a wonderful place to cook in. If you ever get a chance to visit you will recognize the kitchen!

Long before we arrive on the set I have written every recipe for the show. My friends think it's great because there's a non-stop dinner party at my house as I

test the recipes in advance. Sometimes, though, I'm not ready: the day we made omelets I had to try five times before I got one just right! And then there's always the chance that I'm going to change my mind at the last minute and rework a recipe. There are a few shows that include me making something for the first time ever while the cameras are rolling. That's how you make a director nervous!

Before we roll the cameras on a take we carefully plot out the action. Every ingredient is weighed and positioned just so. We figure out which tools we will need and choreograph some of the action. When everything seems ready we do a quick rehearsal known as the "run through for time." This allows the camera operators to figure out their angles and get some sense of what's coming. If we are cooking a recipe that requires a long period of time we will have it prepared all the way through to several stages of doneness so that we can flow from one stage to the next seamlessly. On television things happen a lot quicker than they do in reality!

When everything is ready the director counts down and we're off! When I see the little red light flash on the camera I know we're rolling and somehow, magically, everything else disappears and it's just me and the lens having some fun. It's a neat feeling and is perfectly natural (although the first few times it was anything but natural!). I don't practice my lines, so everything I say is essentially spontaneous. I often know what I want to say but usually have no idea how I will say it, and the

best moments are the unplanned ones. Throughout the take I can hear the director in a tiny monitor hidden in my ear. He lets me know how we're doing and reminds me of anything I may have forgotten. Meanwhile the kitchen assistants are buzzing around me, looking busy and trying not to stare at the cameras, while above my head no fewer than 35 high-powered lights are beaming down like artificial suns. Sometimes we stop briefly and start again from another camera angle. This allows us to edit what's known as "time compression." I may be puréeing a sauce that would normally take two or three minutes, so with careful planning we are able to show the beginning and the end and make it go much faster. Then before you know it I'm saying, "Let's take a break and when we come back . . ."

When something goes wrong you have to roll with it! Once I poured a simmering hot sauce into a blender and turned it on. Boom! It took us half an hour to clean the carrot sauce off everything while I walked around wondering whatever possessed me to do something I would never do in a real kitchen. Another time I reached into the oven for some roast garlic and came out with a roast chicken we had forgotten was still in the oven! Oh well, that's why we have bloopers!

As soon as the take is over we swing into wild high gear. We have about 15 minutes to set up for the next take. It's hard work and this is where the kitchen assistants are invaluable. It takes a lot of careful planning to roll over the set quickly; usually something that I've just done has already been done several times so that we can show it right away at its next logical step. From start to finish, each four-minute segment that you see on TV takes about one hour to execute. We film two complete shows each day on the kitchen set!

The outside stories take longer and we are usually able to get only one a day done because we have to haul all the gear around in a big truck, setting it up and taking it down throughout the day. It's always so strange to see the polished results on screen because you can never see the 20 people that I can see behind the camera — it just looks like me out for a private stroll!

Once we are done filming there is still thousands of hours of work left. The digital editing process takes months of hard work. We also have to go to a recording studio to record the "voice-overs" that are sometimes part of the story telling. I watch every show during the final editing stages to make sure that everything makes sense, although now and then a mistake will slip by. Watch closely and you might see the show that features a large bowl magically appearing and disappearing on the counter behind me!

The Inn Chef is very much a team effort, with a large cast of talented professionals each playing an integral role and having an impact on the final product. It's just my job to smile at the camera!

The Inn Chef Online:
www.innchef.com

◇

Technology is amazing! I am thrilled at the impact that the computer revolution has had on cuisine in general and specifically my kitchen.

even have a PC station in my new kitchen that all my cooks and I use every day. Have you ever cruised the web and seen the awesome variety of food-related sites? In one hour, I can check the daily menu postings of some of the finest restaurants in North America, order purple asparagus seeds, consult with a chef a thousand miles away about a tricky technique, add to my cookbook collection, and of course check out the guest book of my web page, www.innchef.com.

Next time you're on the web, check out our site. It's loaded with cool stuff! Besides recipes, we have a color photo of every dish we've ever made as well as behind-the-scenes photos and contact information for all the places we've visited. And while you're there leave a message in the guest book!

I also enjoy reading and responding to all the e-mail we get every week about the show. It's a great way to stay in touch with you, our audience. Your perception of our efforts is important to us and always entertaining. I'm amazed at the variety of e-mail I get. Here are some of my favorites and my answers.

Dear Chef Michael Smith,
I am a cook at a restaurant in my hometown. I really enjoy my job and would like to be a chef like you. What career advice do you have for me?
— Thomas

Dear Thomas,
I'm glad you're enjoying your path through the greatest career on earth. Take your time along the way, because when you become a chef you won't have as much time to learn and experience the things you can now. I strongly suggest you consider attending a culinary school. I did, and it defined my career forever. Before you go I also suggest you work for at least a year in a reputable restaurant for a real chef. You will gain invaluable experience that will help you get even more out of your time spent in school. Keep an open mind and take the time to travel and dine whenever you can. Good luck!
— Chef Michael

Dearest Michael,
Are you married?
— Heather

Dear Heather,
Not yet. Are you interested?
— Chef Michael

Dear Michael,
Your show is the best on television, better than every other show on every other channel.
— Ralph E. Smith

Dear Dad,
Thanks for watching. I love you!
— Michael

Dear Michael,
Is the Inn a real place? How can we visit?
— Dan and Eve Statler

Dear Dan and Eve,
The Inn at Bay Fortune is the premier country house on Prince Edward Island. It is nestled in the countryside to the east of Charlottetown and overlooks Bay Fortune and the ocean beyond. It is a beautiful place to visit and relax and of course to dine. For more information check out their web site at www.innatbayfortune.com or call (902) 687-3745. If you ever make it to PEI, don't miss it!
— Chef Michael

Dear Michael,
How tall are you?
— An interested viewer

Dear interested viewer,
I am the world's tallest chef, which is why I can't wear the traditional chef's hat! I stand six feet eight inches tall, with the wind at my back, and on a clear day I can see my clogs!
— Chef Michael

Dear Michael,
Do you have a recipe for hummingbird pie?
— Margaret Ann Smith

Dear Mom,
No, but you do! I love you!
— Michael

Dear Chef Michael,

I am an avid cook and really enjoy your show. What books do you suggest for my cookbook collection?
— Amy Dugan

Dear Amy,

I owe much of my success to the inspiration I have gleaned from my voracious reading and expansive library. Here are the books I consider the cornerstones of any good cookbook collection:

1. *Le Guide Culinaire,* by Auguste Escoffier, is the book that started it all, the first real cookbook for professionals, a must-read.

2. *On Food and Cooking,* by Harold McGee, describes in an easy-to-understand way the science behind good cooking.

3. *The New Joy of Cooking,* by Irma Rombauer, Marion Rombauer, and Ethan Becker, is the single most comprehensive cookbook I know of.

4. *The Pie and Pastry Bible,* by Rose Levy Beranbaum, is a must have for pastry fans.

5. *Bread Alone,* by Daniel Leader, the baker's guru!

6. *The Art of Eating,* by M.F.K. Fisher, a delightful read by a wonderful writer.

7. *The Physiology of Taste,* by Brillat-Savarin, is an 1825 book that delves into the psychology of cuisine.

8. *The Professional Chef,* by the faculty of the Culinary Institute of America, the all-encompassing textbook from my school days.

9. Any cookbook written by a restaurant chef. I have more than a hundred. They give me insight into the style of other cooks.

10. *Open Kitchen,* by Me, my first book!
— Chef Michael

Dear Michael,

What is your favorite thing to cook?
— Lana Preassio

Dear Lana,

It's hard to say that any one thing is more enjoyable than any other in cooking, but I seem to get the most satisfaction out of braising. To be able to take the toughest piece of meat and elevate it to cuisine is miraculous, and a braise always tastes good. In fact, I dream of opening a restaurant that serves nothing but great braises like beef stew!
— Chef Michael

Let's Get Cooking

◇

When I wrote my first cookbook, *Open Kitchen,* I put a lot of thought into the definition of its recipes.

I considered how they should be conceived, what information they should include, and how they should be followed. I imagined the contrasts between my state-of-the-art cuisine studio and the realities of a home kitchen. I even pondered the inevitable evolution of the recipes before forging ahead.

I discovered that there were certain basic concepts that were of great importance, a state of defined readiness. My conclusions were sound, so I've updated and included them here to help you get the most out of this book whether you're headed for the kitchen or an easy chair!

One aspect of my recipes that I am unable to include is their creation. I can describe for you the many and varied influences on my cuisine and even the inspiration behind its flavors, but I can't impart the precise symbiotic flow that defines a cook and his ingredients as they progress together. Only you can do that as you follow the words I have written. As you do, the recipes in this book become what I have intended them to be all along: mere suggestions and guideposts. I'm only writing; you complete the equation by touching, smelling,

tasting, and cooking the ingredients. You will achieve the full realization of these recipes by your ability to grow them, change them, modify them, or otherwise personalize them. In fact, just cooking them once makes them yours, just as they first became mine through the experiences of my kitchen. I urge you to seize the opportunity to create your own cuisine!

As you gain experience in the nuances of your ingredients and the simple techniques that make them shine, you will have the opportunity to create on your own. I suggest you use these recipes as a mere starting point for your own culinary expedition — change the flavors to suit your own whims. For instance, many of the herbs used are interchangeable and any evolution will profoundly change the character of the dish.

As you evolve your cuisine, consider how the flavors mingle within a presentation. I am very careful to match complementary flavors on every plate. What may seem arbitrary is actually a precise balance of ingredients that work well together. This is a hallmark of my cuisine and is easily understood. Taste the magic that tomato and basil make together. Now try to recreate that harmony when creating on your own.

Generally I begin with two dominant flavors that I then bridge with a third. Each can enter the plate as a component of the main protein, vegetables, sauce, or garnish. The individual recipes that come together must create a cohesive whole on the plate. They don't stand alone; they interact with their neighbors in a sort of culinary teamwork that elevates all. Obviously there are other ingredients at work, but they form the base that allows the dominant flavors to shine.

Of special note: In the recipes eggs are large, butter is unsalted, cream is heavy, meats and fish are perfect, fruit is ripe, vegetables are garden grown, herbs and spices are fresh, all salt is coarse sea salt and pepper is freshly ground black pepper. Every ingredient should represent an opportunity for excellence.

When a recipe calls for a ring mold, I use PVC or ABS pipe from the hardware store that's trimmed and polished. A good size to have on hand is 3 or 3½ inches/ 8 or 9 cm wide by 1½ inches/4 cm tall.

If you want your cuisine to reflect the spirit of my kitchen, the following points are worth incorporating into your repertoire.

◇ You may call the dishes whatever you wish. My titles tend to include the main flavors and cooking techniques. I try not to give away any clues to the presentation or "look" of the plate, since I like to keep that a surprise. Simplify or exaggerate as you wish.

◇ Read each menu item thoroughly before you begin the preparation. Get a sense of the timing of the recipes that make up the plate and have your ingredients — your mise-en-place — ready.

◇ Organize your work space, and have ready a supply of plates and bowls to hold the various ingredients of a recipe until they are needed. The pros don't have piles of things lying around waiting to be used; instead, everything is treated with respect and carefully stored awaiting its role in the production.

◇ If you really want to duplicate my cuisine, stock your kitchen with great ingredients. Spend a little more if need be. Remember, you have control of most of the flavor of a dish as you gather its components. The results will reflect the quality of the ingredients you use.

◇ Use your good culinary sense. Many variables in your environment, such as your equipment, tools, ingredients, and kitchen, will affect your efforts. Use these variables to your advantage.

◇ The recipes in this book reflect only one moment in the evolution of my cuisine. Don't treat them as static. Use them, modify them, let them evolve in your kitchen.

◇ Use your best judgment when seasoning with salt and pepper. It is often impossible to establish the exact amounts needed. There are too many variables. I suggest you season where indicated and taste, if possible, to judge the seasoning. A good cook often seasons throughout the cooking process. In fact, I often sprinkle on some crunchy sea salt at the last second.

◇ Taste as you go. The changing flavors that you will witness are part of cuisine and are an opportunity for insight — pay attention!

◇ Focus on your craftsmanship. Watch the ingredients as they evolve, as you follow the preparation steps. Adjust their progress if needed. Be patient and precise. Sweat the details.

◇ The timing sections indicate the timing needed for the preparation of each menu item. Very often several of these recipes can be under way simultaneously. If so, follow the instructions carefully. Within a presentation, recipes have been arranged in the order they are to be cooked. (However, because of space considerations, occasionally it was necessary to print recipes in a different order.)

◇ Have fun with the presentation of these menu items. This type of cuisine inspires artful presentation. Follow the guidelines and add your own flair.

◇ Before you go to the plate, make sure your guests are ready. Nothing is worse than having cuisine wait to be enjoyed.

◇ Above all enjoy yourself. Cooking is fun! Invite a friend to join you, put on some good music, pour a glass of wine, relax, and let your cuisine flow.

All in all, some pretty straightforward advice. Like most art forms, cooking celebrates the process. The art is in the motion, the fluid dance of the cook and her ingredients. These tips will help to create the kitchen aesthetic of artful cuisine.

Caramel and Horseradish Apple Soups
with Sharp Cheddar Fritters
and Spicy Apple Chutney

A classic group of flavors brought together in an extravagant reunion of swirling apple and crisp cheddar. Together, two distinct soups and their presentation create a memorable tasting experience from familiar flavors.

◇ 6 SERVINGS ◇

TIMING: MAKE THE CHUTNEY AND REFRIGERATE OVERNIGHT. │ MAKE THE FRITTER BATTER AND REFRIGERATE FOR 60 MINUTES.
│ REMOVE THE CHUTNEY FROM THE REFRIGERATOR TO WARM. │ MAKE THE SOUPS. │ COOK THE FRITTERS AND WARM THE SOUPS.

Spicy Apple Chutney

1 cup / 250 mL sugar

½ cup / 125 mL water

2 large onions, chopped (about 4 cups / 1 L)

2 Granny Smith apples, peeled, cored, and medium chopped (about 3 cups / 750 mL)

½ cup / 125 mL cider vinegar

1 teaspoon / 5 mL Bay Fortune seasoning (page 40)

1 teaspoon / 5 mL ground allspice

1 teaspoon / 5 mL Tabasco® pepper sauce

½ teaspoon / 2 mL salt

In a medium, heavy saucepan over low heat, melt the sugar and water, swirling gently just to dissolve it. Increase the heat to high and boil the syrup, gently swirling the caramel as it begins to color. When it reaches an even deep golden brown, add the onion (the caramel will bubble up). Stir and cook the onion in the caramel until most of the liquid has evaporated.

Add the apples, vinegar, Bay Fortune seasoning, allspice, Tabasco®, and salt and bring to a simmer. Cook for 5 minutes over medium heat, stirring gently. Remove the chutney from the heat, let cool, place in a storage container, and refrigerate overnight. Remove the chutney from the refrigerator in time to reach room temperature before serving.

Sharp Cheddar Fritters

Sift together the flour, salt, and baking powder in a bowl. In a medium saucepan, bring the milk and butter to a simmer. Add the flour mixture to the milk mixture all at once and stir vigorously until a smooth paste is formed.

Place the flour paste in a food processor. Add the cheese and egg, and process until thoroughly incorporated and the mixture forms a smooth paste again. Remove the batter, place it in a storage container, and refrigerate for 60 minutes or so. (Meanwhile, prepare the soups.)

Preheat the oven to 300°F/150°C.

In a high-sided pan, heat the oil until it reaches 365°F/185°C. Using 2 teaspoons, form the batter into evenly shaped fritters (12 in total) no more than 1 inch/2.5 cm thick, and drop them carefully into the hot oil. Don't fill the pan. Fry just a few fritters at a time, turning them frequently so they brown on all sides. When the fritters have plumped up and are golden brown, remove them with a slotted spoon and drain them on paper towels. Heat the oil again, and continue forming and frying fritters until the batter is all used. Reheat the fritters in the oven for a few minutes, and serve immediately.

The batter is easier to work with when it has been left to stand for an hour. Before you begin frying, practice forming the fritters until they are a consistent shape. The fritters should be tapered and have pointed ends, and vaguely resemble a football. Any shape will work; the trick is to be consistent.

¼ cup / 60 mL all-purpose flour

½ teaspoon / 2 mL salt

¼ teaspoon / 1 mL baking powder

¼ cup / 60 mL milk

2 tablespoons / 25 mL butter

1 cup / 250 mL shredded sharp cheddar cheese

1 egg, beaten

4 cups / 1 L vegetable oil

Caramel Apple Soup

½ cup / 125 mL sugar

¼ cup / 60 mL water

1 large onion, chopped (about 2 cups / 500 mL)

2 Granny Smith apples, peeled, cored, and chopped (about 3 cups / 750 mL)

3 cups / 750 mL cider

2 teaspoons / 10 mL salt

1 ½ teaspoons / 7 mL cinnamon

In a medium, heavy saucepan over low heat, melt the sugar and water, swirling gently just to dissolve it. Increase the heat to high and boil the syrup, gently swirling the caramel as it begins to color. When it reaches an even deep golden brown, add the onion (the caramel will bubble up). Stir and cook the onion in the caramel until the caramel is completely dissolved. Continue cooking until the moisture in the onion evaporates and the onion begins to brown.

When the onion has caramelized, add the apples, cider, salt, and cinnamon and bring the mixture to a boil. Cover the pot, reduce the heat to a simmer, and cook for 20 minutes.

Pour the soup into a blender and purée thoroughly. Strain through a fine-mesh strainer, return it to the wiped clean saucepan, and set aside.

Warm the soup, stirring frequently, while the fritters are being cooked. The soup may also be made ahead and refrigerated.

This soup will benefit from being stored overnight in the refrigerator; the flavors will combine and become more pronounced. Reheat it slowly in a saucepan, stirring frequently. A food processor can also be used to purée the soup, but it won't be as smooth.

Horseradish Apple Soup

In a large pot, sauté the onion in the butter until the onion is translucent. Add the apples, apple juice, wine, horseradish, salt, and nutmeg and bring to a boil. Reduce the heat until the soup is just simmering, then cover the pot with a tight-fitting lid. Cook for 20 minutes, or until the apples are very soft.

Pour the soup into a blender and purée thoroughly. Strain through a fine-mesh strainer and set aside.

Warm the soup, stirring frequently, while the fritters are being cooked. The soup may also be made ahead and refrigerated.

1 large onion, chopped (about 2 cups / 500 mL)

1 tablespoon / 15 mL butter

2 Granny Smith apples, peeled, cored, and chopped (about 3 cups / 750 mL)

2 cups / 500 mL apple juice

1 cup / 250 mL Chardonnay

½ cup / 125 mL prepared horseradish

2 teaspoons / 10 mL salt

1 teaspoon / 5 mL ground nutmeg

The Plate!

Use 6 warm broad, shallow soup bowls. Rest the bottom of each soup bowl on the edge of an overturned plate so that the bowl is slightly tilted. Ladle one of the soups into the lower part of the bowl. As you tilt the bowl back to level with your other hand, ladle the second soup into the other side of the bowl. Place a scoop of chutney in the center of each bowl and top with 2 fritters. Serve with a spoon!

◈ HORSERADISH ◈

The ancients, who tended to think of it mainly as a medicinal plant, held horseradish in high regard. Native to central Europe, it spread throughout the continent in Renaissance times. Today we value its root for its sharp mustard-like flavor. A perennial plant, it is usually grown from root cuttings. Once planted it will dominate its part of the garden and is almost impossible to eradicate.

Roast Corn Soup with Spicy Shrimp, Jack Corn Fritters, a Cactus, and a Southwestern Swirl

The Southwest is a treasure trove of ingredients and precise culinary traditions.
This soup is a great way to show some of them off. El Paso, here we come!

◆ 6 SERVINGS ◆

TIMING: MAKE THE SOUP, THE TWO CREAM SWIRLS, THE FRITTER BATTER, AND THE TORTILLA CACTUS AHEAD OF TIME.
| AT THE LAST MINUTE FRY THE FRITTERS AND ROAST THE SHRIMP.

Roast Corn Soup

6 ears corn, shucked

4 ounces / 125 g fresh chorizo sausage, chopped

4 tablespoons / 60 mL corn oil

1 large onion, minced

4 cloves garlic, minced

1 tablespoon / 15 mL ground cumin

6 cups / 1.5 L rich chicken broth

⅔ cup / 150 mL yellow cornmeal

Salt and pepper

Stand the ears of corn on their ends and using a sharp knife slice the kernels from the cob. Do not cut into the woody cob or leave behind any of the kernels. Reserve the cobs. Reserve 1 cup/250 mL of the corn for the fritters.

Place the chorizo in a large pot with the oil and remaining corn kernels. Stir the mixture frequently over medium to high heat as the corn begins to caramelize. When the corn is a uniform deep golden color, add the onion, garlic, and cumin and cook a few minutes longer. Add the chicken broth and bring to a simmer.

Place the cobs in the chicken broth and continue simmering, covered, for 30 minutes. Remove the cobs and discard them.

Whisking constantly, add a slow, steady stream of the cornmeal to the broth. Continue stirring as the broth begins to thicken, about 15 minutes. Season to taste with salt and pepper, and set aside.

Reheat the soup over medium heat while the fritters are being cooked.

The cob of a corn ear is equally as flavorful as the kernels but that flavor needs to be extracted through simmering. Caramelizing the corn is the key to the deep corn flavor of this soup.

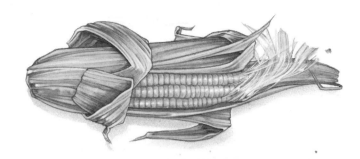

Jack Corn Fritters

Place the milk and cornmeal in a small saucepan over medium heat. Stir constantly as the mixture thickens and eventually forms a ball. Place the cornmeal ball in a food processor.

Add the eggs, flour, and baking powder and process until smooth. Add the cheese and process until smooth. Season to taste with salt and pepper. Add the reserved corn and the chives; pulse just to stir. The batter may be prepared to this point and refrigerated.

In a countertop deep-fryer or deep pot with 4 inches/10 cm of oil heated to 370°F/185°C, fry several large spoonfuls of batter at a time for a total of 12. Fry just until the fritters are golden brown and crisp. Drain the fritters on paper towels.

Cooking the cornmeal quickly softens it so that it blends better with the other ingredients into a stronger fritter batter. Corn's moisture varies; add some flour to the batter to thicken it if needed.

½ cup / 125 mL milk

¼ cup / 60 mL yellow cornmeal

2 eggs

¼ cup / 60 mL all-purpose flour

½ teaspoon / 2 mL baking powder

1 cup / 250 mL shredded sharp Monterey Jack cheese

Salt and pepper

Reserved corn kernels from the soup

¼ cup / 60 mL snipped chives

Lime Cream

Place the lime and cream in a small saucepan. Bring the mixture to a simmer.

Simmer until reduced by half. Place the mixture in a blender with the cilantro and purée until very smooth. Season to taste with salt and pepper, then strain through a fine-mesh strainer. Reserve in a squeeze bottle.

Make sure the cilantro leaves are clean — they are often sandy, and even one grain will ruin your soup!

Zest and juice of 4 limes

1 cup / 250 mL heavy cream

½ cup / 125 mL cilantro leaves

Salt and pepper

Ancho Cream

1 red pepper, chopped

1 cup / 250 mL heavy cream

1 ancho pepper

Salt and pepper

Place the red pepper and cream in a small saucepan. Bring the mixture to a simmer.

Meanwhile, warm the ancho pepper briefly in a 400°F/200°C oven or microwave just to soften it. Cut it open and remove the seeds. Discard the seeds and the stem. Add the pepper to the cream.

Continue simmering the mixture until the cream is reduced by half. In a blender, purée the mixture until very smooth. Season to taste with salt and pepper, then strain through a fine-mesh strainer. Reserve in a squeeze bottle.

The dry pepper needs to simmer long enough to soften so it will purée.

Tortilla Cactus

1 corn tortilla

Cut the tortilla into 6 (3 to 5-inch/8 to 12 cm long) cactus shapes with a cookie cutter or knife. Fry them until crisp in a deep-fryer or in a deep pot with several inches of oil heated to 370°F/185°C. Drain them on paper towels until cool and reserve them in an airtight container until needed.

Try cutting the tortilla into long, thin strips, then frying them.

Spicy Shrimp

Toss together the sugar and seasonings. Preheat a lightly oiled cast-iron skillet over high heat. Dredge the shrimp in the mixture and place in one layer in the skillet. Pan-roast about 5 minutes until the seasonings turn brown and the shrimp is firm and pink. Serve immediately.

You may use headless shrimp, which will cook a bit quicker. If so use 2 or 3 — depending on size — for each guest. Try experimenting with other spices.

2 tablespoons / 25 mL sugar

2 tablespoons / 25 mL ground cumin

2 tablespoons / 25 mL ground chiles or chili powder

2 tablespoons / 25 mL paprika

Salt and pepper to taste

6 large shrimp, heads on

The Plate!

Ladle ⅔ cup / 150 mL of the hot soup into each of 6 heated wide, shallow soup bowls. Add a tight concentric pattern of the two squeeze sauces, alternating one within the other. Draw the tip of a small blade through them from the center out to feather their edges. Position two of the fritters with a shrimp in each bowl. Garnish with cilantro sprigs and a tortilla cactus. Serve with a whoop!

Cilantro sprigs

❖ CORN ❖

One of the New World's most important agricultural commodities, corn is second only to wheat in prominence. Connoisseurs prefer to have a pot of water boiling before picking the corn, as it begins to convert its sugars into starch as soon as it is picked. If you stand in a corn field on a still night you can actually hear it growing. The distinctive rustling sound is a result of its expanding leaves rubbing over each other.

Saffron Oyster Stew with Chive Essence
and Oyster Fritters

Many recipes innocently obscure — or deliberately hide — the briny essence of an oyster.
Not this one! Here the sea's mineral flavors are framed by the delicate touch of saffron and fresh chives.

◇ 4 SERVINGS ◇

TIMING: MAKE THE CHIVE ESSENCE UP TO 5 DAYS AHEAD. | MAKE THE OYSTER STEW 30 MINUTES AHEAD AND
LET IT REST WHILE MAKING THE FRITTER BATTER. | REHEAT AND SEASON THE STEW AS YOU FRY THE FRITTERS.

Chive Essence

1 cup / 250 mL chopped chives

1 cup / 250 mL extra virgin olive oil

Purée the chives and oil thoroughly in a blender.

Place the purée in a small saucepan and bring to a simmer over medium heat. Simmer for 1 minute.

Strain the oil through a fine-mesh strainer and refrigerate.

If any water has settled below the oil, freeze the oil in a shallow bowl and then remove the oil from the frozen water.

Heating the chives deepens their color to a beautiful emerald. You may replace the chives with the green tops of green onion or leek.

Saffron Oyster Stew

24 oysters

2 tablespoons / 25 mL butter

1 large onion, minced

1 tablespoon / 15 mL minced garlic

Shuck the oysters, reserving the liquid. Set aside the oysters for the fritters.

In a large saucepan over medium-high heat, sauté the onions in the butter until they begin to turn golden. Add the garlic and sauté for a few more minutes. Add the Chardonnay and simmer briefly.

Stir in the cream, the reserved oyster liquid, and the saffron threads and bring to a simmer. Simmer for 10 minutes. Remove from the heat and let rest for 30 minutes. Gently reheat the stew while making the fritters. Season with salt and pepper to taste.

1 cup / 250 mL Chardonnay

2 cups / 500 mL heavy cream

1 teaspoon / 5 mL saffron threads

Salt and pepper

Be patient; the gentle, even browning of the onions mellows their flavor. Add the garlic last, as it browns faster than onions and may burn. Allowing the saffron to steep for half an hour in the warm flavor base allows its flavors to deepen.

Oyster Fritters

In a deep saucepan, begin heating 4 inches/10 cm of frying oil to 365°F/185°C.

Pour the beer into a mixing bowl and add the baking powder with a pinch of salt and pepper. Stir in enough flour to form a batter that will adhere to the oysters.

Dip each oyster into the batter and fry a few at a time in the hot oil. Turn them as they fry. When they are golden brown remove them with a slotted spoon and let drain briefly on paper towels. Keep them warm while you fry the remaining fritters.

Oil for frying

1 bottle lager or ale (not a darker beer)

1 teaspoon / 5 mL baking powder

Salt and pepper

½ to 1 cup / 125 to 250 mL all-purpose or other flour

24 oysters

Don't crowd the oil, and make sure the oil remains at 365° F/185° C after the fritters are added. Too hot and you burn the fritters; too low and the fritters absorb more of the frying fat and turn greasy.

The Plate!

Ladle the saffron stew into 4 warm soup bowls. Add 6 oyster fritters to each bowl and drizzle with chive essence. Garnish with chives and serve immediately. Serve with a sly grin!

Chives

Island Blue Mussel and Sweet Potato Chowder with Bay Fortune Spiced Bread Sticks, Spicy Butter, and a Stuffed Onion

I created this recipe for a dinner party at my dad's house when I was still a student at culinary school. He's now an avid watcher of *The Inn Chef* and remembers the world debut of this soup. His down-south sweet potatoes and my up-north mussels are still a hit in Manhattan, where he lives!

◇ 6 SERVINGS ◇

TIMING: MAKE THE SPICY BUTTER, CHOWDER, AND BREAD STICKS AHEAD. | ROAST THE ONIONS AND REHEAT JUST BEFORE NEEDED.

Bay Fortune Seasoning

1 ounce / 25 g ground bay leaf

1 ounce / 25 g ground coriander

1 ounce / 25 g ground fennel

Mix together all the ingredients and store in an airtight container in a cool, dark place.

Use ½ teaspoon/2 mL of the mixture when a recipe calls for a bay leaf.

Spicy Butter

2 tablespoons / 25 mL butter

2 tablespoons / 25 mL heavy cream

2 tablespoons / 25 mL molasses

1 ½ teaspoons / 7 mL Tabasco® pepper sauce

¼ teaspoon / 1 mL ground allspice

¼ teaspoon / 1 mL ground cloves

Put the butter, cream, molasses, Tabasco®, allspice, and cloves in a small saucepan and bring the mixture to a simmer, stirring frequently. Remove from the heat, and allow the mixture to cool to room temperature. Transfer the butter to a squeeze bottle.

Island Blue Mussel and Sweet Potato Chowder

Place the mussels and water in a saucepan with a tight-fitting lid. Place the pot over high heat and steam the mussels for 10 to 12 minutes until the shells open. Discard any mussels that don't open. Remove the meat from the shells and set the meat aside for the stuffed onion, and reserve some shells to use in the presentation. Strain and reserve the mussel broth.

In a large pot, sauté the onion in the butter over high heat for about 10 minutes. Stir frequently, and turn the heat down slightly every few minutes to prevent burning. Add the garlic and continue cooking until the onion is golden brown. Add the carrot, sweet potato, milk, cream, Bay Fortune seasoning, salt, Tabasco®, and 1 cup/250 mL of the mussel broth. Bring the mixture to a boil, reduce the heat to low, cover the pot, and let it simmer gently for 30 minutes. Stir frequently to prevent scorching on the bottom of the pot. (While it is simmering, make the spicy butter.) After 30 minutes, check the vegetables for doneness. If they are soft, remove the pot from the heat. If they are still slightly al dente, simmer a few minutes longer or until done.

Purée the soup thoroughly in a blender, and strain through a fine-mesh strainer. If necessary, adjust the consistency of the soup with the remaining mussel broth. The soup should be pleasantly thick but not goopy.

Return the soup to the pot and heat it, stirring frequently. Serve immediately.

It is important not to overcook the mussels. Steam them for only a few minutes after the shells have opened; the mussels should stay plump and juicy. Let the reserved mussel liquid stand, and some sediment may settle to the bottom of the pot. Carefully pour out the liquid, leaving the harmless silt behind. Using a blender is the best way to get a perfectly smooth soup, but a food processor will work almost as well.

5 pounds / 2.2 kg island blue mussels

4 tablespoons / 60 mL water

1 large onion, chopped (about 2 cups / 500 mL)

4 tablespoons / 60 mL butter

4 cloves garlic, chopped

2 medium carrots, grated

2 medium sweet potatoes, grated

2 cups / 500 mL milk

1 cup / 250 mL heavy cream

1 teaspoon / 5 mL Bay Fortune seasoning (page 40)

1 teaspoon / 5 mL salt

1 teaspoon / 5 mL Tabasco® pepper sauce

Bread Sticks

1 ¼ cups / 300 mL bread flour

1 teaspoon / 5 mL sugar

½ teaspoon / 2 mL salt

¾ cup / 175 mL water

1 teaspoon / 5 mL Bay Fortune
seasoning (page 40)

1 egg

Coarse sea salt

Preheat the oven to 400°F/200°C.

Place the flour, sugar, salt, ½ cup/25 mL of the water, and the Bay Fortune
seasoning in a food processor fitted with a plastic dough blade. Process the dough
until it becomes a cohesive mass. Let the dough rest for several minutes.

Pinch off 1 ounce/25 g pieces of the dough. On a lightly floured surface, roll
them out into 6-inch/15 cm sticks with your hands. Make 6 sticks with a small
loop at one end large enough to pass a nickel through. Make 18 sticks altogether.
Arrange on a lightly oiled baking sheet.

Whisk together the egg and remaining ¼ cup/60 mL of water and brush each
stick with the egg wash. Sprinkle the sticks with coarse sea salt. Bake until golden
brown, about 20 to 30 minutes. Cool bread sticks on a rack.

*The loops on the ends of the bread sticks should be just large enough to hold the ends of
2 sticks. There's no yeast in the dough so it will barely rise.*

Stuffed Onions

6 small onions

1 tablespoon / 15 mL extra virgin olive oil

Salt and pepper to taste

Reserved mussels

1 ½ cups / 375 mL celery leaves, finely
sliced

Preheat the oven to 400°F/200°C.

Peel the onions and trim off the root end very close to the roots. Cut the other
end off about ½ inch from the top, leaving a larger cross section exposed. Using a
melon-baller, hollow out the onion. Reserve the scooped onion for another use.

Rub the insides and outsides of the hollow onions with the olive oil and salt and
pepper and arrange them in a small roasting pan.

Bake the onions for 20 to 30 minutes until they brown slightly.

Mix the mussels and celery leaves together. Season the mixture and stuff it into the onions.

Just before serving the soup, reheat the onions in a microwave oven or in the still warm oven until hot.

Chop and brown the leftover onion and add it to the mussel mixture. One onion, two flavors!

The Plate!

If necessary, reheat the soup. Ladle ⅔ cup/150 mL of it into each of 6 hot large soup or pasta plates set on underlying plates with the reserved mussel shells poking out. Squeeze some of the spicy butter around the outside of the soup. If there is any leftover mussel mix from the stuffed onions, spoon it into the center of the bowl. Place a celery leaf in the center of the soup and perch a stuffed onion on top of it. Fashion a standing tripod out of the bread sticks by inserting 2 sticks into the stick with the loop and arrange over the soup bowl. Serve with a flourish!

Reserved mussel shells

Celery leaves

◆ MUSSELS ◆

Mussels are native to the cold waters of the Atlantic and Pacific, although today they are most commonly aquacultured. Because they are grown suspended off the bottom, they are usually grit free. If a mussel refuses to close its shell when squeezed, discard it — it's dead. In Belgium they are so common that instead of hot dog wagons, mussel wagons are found plying city streets.

Lovage Clam Chowder
with a Potato-Crusted Crab Cake,
Pickled Cucumber, and Lovage Chips

As a kid I was an accomplished connoisseur of clam chowder and became a life-long fan of its many versions. The intense celery-like flavor and brilliant color of the herb lovage star in this new-age clam version. Crisp potatoes and a crab cake complement the seaside character of the dish.

◇ 6 SERVINGS ◇

TIMING: MAKE THE LOVAGE CHIPS THE DAY BEFORE. | MAKE THE PICKLED CUCUMBERS AND LET REST OVERNIGHT OR FOR A FEW HOURS. | FORM AND REFRIGERATE THE CRAB CAKES A FEW HOURS AHEAD. | MAKE THE CHOWDER AND BREAD AND BROWN THE CRAB CAKES.

Pickled Cucumbers

Zest and juice of 1 lemon

4 tablespoons / 60 mL extra virgin olive oil

1 tablespoon / 15 mL whole grain mustard

¼ cup / 60 mL capers

¼ cup / 60 mL minced red onion

1 cup / 250 mL julienned cucumber

Salt and pepper

Mix together the lemon zest and juice, oil, mustard, capers, and red onions until well combined. Add the cucumber and toss well. Season to taste with salt and pepper. Let the pickles rest for several hours or overnight before serving.

As the cucumbers rest and pickle they shrink, giving off water and diluting the flavor. For a different flavor effect, add double the lemons and spices.

Lovage Chips

1 large potato (about 6 ounces / 175 g), baked

1 tablespoon / 15 mL butter

2 egg whites

1 tablespoon / 15 mL all-purpose flour

1 tablespoon / 15 mL chopped lovage

Preheat the oven to 350°F/180°C. Lightly oil a nonstick baking sheet.

Scoop the flesh from the potato and discard the skin. Combine all the ingredients in a food processor and process until a smooth batter forms.

Use a sharp knife to cut a 4-inch/10 cm triangle template out of a food-safe plastic lid or milk carton.

Using the template, spread 1 tablespoon/15 mL of the dough evenly on the baking sheet until you have 12 triangles. Bake until golden brown, about 10 minutes. The chips will brown unevenly, so turn the pan a few times during baking. Remove any chips that are done before their mates.

Serve immediately or keep for a day in an airtight container.

The potato must be thoroughly baked. If it feels creamy inside when squeezed, it will have lost enough moisture to make this batter work. Take the time to spread the batter evenly so it cooks evenly.

Potato-Crusted Crab Cakes

Preheat the oven to 350°F/180°C.

Steam the potatoes until tender, then pass them through a food mill onto a baking sheet. Spread them evenly on the sheet. Dry the potatoes in the oven for 10 minutes.

In a bowl whisk 1 of the eggs. Add the oven-dried potatoes, crab meat, and chives. Season to taste with salt and pepper. Combine the ingredients gently until they are well mixed.

Form 6 cylindrical crab cakes. Press them firmly together as you form them. The cakes should be made to this point and refrigerated, covered, several hours.

In a shallow dish whisk together the remaining 3 eggs. Have ready in two separate dishes the flour and mashed potato flakes.

Bread the crab cakes by first rolling them in the flour, then dipping them in egg wash, and finally rolling them in potato flakes.

1 pound / 500 g potatoes, peeled and quartered

4 eggs

1 cup / 250 mL crab meat

¼ cup / 60 mL snipped chives

Salt and pepper

All-purpose flour and instant mashed potato flakes for breading

2 tablespoons / 25 mL butter

continued > >

Preheat the oven to 400°F/200°C. In an ovenproof nonstick skillet over medium-high heat, melt the butter. Cook the crab cakes until evenly browned all over. Finish cooking in the oven for 10 minutes. Serve immediately.

Lovage Clam Chowder

2 tablespoons / 25 mL butter

1 cup / 250 mL chopped onions

2 cloves garlic, chopped

1 cup / 250 mL dry vermouth

2 cups / 500 mL heavy cream

1 cup / 250 mL crab broth or clam juice

1 cup / 250 mL grated peeled potato

1 cup / 250 mL lovage leaves

1 cup / 250 mL chopped green onion tops

1 cup / 250 mL clams

Salt and pepper

Place the butter, onions, and garlic in a heavy saucepan over medium heat and sweat them, stirring, until the onions are slightly browned, about 10 minutes.

Add the vermouth, cream, crab broth, and potato. Bring the mixture to a simmer and cook just long enough to soften the potatoes, about 20 minutes.

Place the lovage and green onions in a blender. Add the soup and blend until very smooth. Strain the soup into a clean saucepan and set aside.

While you cook the crab cakes, add the clams and gently reheat the soup. Season to taste with salt and pepper. Serve immediately. (If you make the soup in advance, much of its green color will be lost.)

Steam the clams just long enough for them to open and heat through; if they begin to shrink they will toughen. Not overheating the herb leaves heightens their color.

The Plate!

Lovage sprigs

Ladle ¾ cup/175 mL of the chowder into each of 6 hot soup bowls. Add a crisp potato cake to the center of each bowl. Top each cake with a spoonful of the pickled cucumbers. Insert two of the lovage chips, point down, into the cucumber and garnish with a lovage sprig. Serve with a swoop!

Brandy Oxtail Consommé with a Morel Mushroom Flan and Foie Gras-Stuffed Morels, with Arugula and Steak Julienne

The art and science of classic consommé technique are reflected in this sophisticated range of flavors. Ribbons of green arugula and tender steak swim in the clear broth, replenishing the flavor lost in the clarifying process. A worthy sacrifice!

◇ 6 SERVINGS ◇

TIMING: MAKE THE OXTAIL CONSOMMÉ THE DAY BEFORE. | MAKE THE FLANS AN HOUR BEFORE SERVING. | MAKE THE STUFFED MORELS WHILE THE FLANS ARE BAKING. | JUST BEFORE SERVING, DRESS THE BOWLS WITH THE ARUGULA AND STEAK JULIENNE AND REHEAT THE CONSOMMÉ.

Foie Gras-Stuffed Morels

Place the foie gras in a small saucepan and add enough wine to cover. Add the onion, celery, carrot, garlic, and bay leaves and bring the mixture to a very low simmer. Simmer for 5 minutes. Remove the foie gras and refrigerate it. Discard the cooking liquid.

Meanwhile, prepare the morels. If they are dried, place them in a small saucepan with 1 cup/250 mL of red wine and bring to a simmer. Simmer just long enough for the morels to absorb all the wine, about 10 to 15 minutes. Remove the morels to a plate and let them rest. If they are fresh, gently sauté them in olive oil or butter just long enough to heat them through. Lightly season the morels with salt and pepper and let rest.

When the foie gras is thoroughly chilled, purée it in a food processor until smooth. Season with salt and pepper. Place the foie gras in a small piping bag fitted with a small tip and fill the mushrooms. Serve immediately or let rest before gently reheating in a microwave.

8 ounces / 250 g fresh foie gras

2 to 3 cups / 500 to 750 mL red wine

½ onion, minced

½ stalk celery, minced

½ carrot, minced

2 cloves garlic, sliced

2 bay leaves

12 large dried or fresh morels

Salt and pepper to taste

To save time sear the foie gras and then stuff it into quickly sautéed morels. Either way the center of the foie gras should be just heated through to minimize fat loss.

Brandy Oxtail Consommé

4 tablespoons / 60 mL butter

2 oxtails (about 2 pounds / 1 kg), chopped into several pieces

4 cups / 1 L Cabernet Sauvignon

8 cups / 2 L water

2 large carrots, peeled and diced

2 large stalks celery, diced

2 large onions, diced

8 cloves garlic, sliced

4 bay leaves

THE SECOND GROUP OF VEGETABLES:

1 small onion, cut into large pieces

1 small carrot, peeled and chopped

1 small stalk celery, chopped

2 large tomatoes

4 stalks fresh parsley

¾ pound / 375 g lean stewing beef, in large pieces

3 egg whites

½ cup / 125 mL brandy

Salt

Melt the butter in a large stockpot over medium-high heat. When it begins to brown add the oxtails and brown them evenly on all sides. Don't burn the butter or the pot! If necessary, turn the heat down slightly. When the pieces are brown, pour off the butter and discard. Replace the oxtails and continue.

Add the wine, water, carrots, celery, onions, garlic, and bay leaves. Bring to a simmer, cover the pot, and cook gently for 3 to 4 hours until the meat is very tender and falls off the bones. As the broth simmers keep topping up the liquid so it just covers the simmering ingredients.

Discard the bones. Strain the broth through a fine-mesh strainer. Chill the soup several hours or overnight to congeal the fat on its surface, then discard the fat.

Bring the broth to a simmer, uncovered. Simmer until the broth has reduced to 6 cups/1.5 L. Let the broth cool to room temperature.

Combine the second group of vegetables in a food processor with the parsley and process until coarsely chopped. Add the stewing beef and process until it is chopped into small pieces. Add the egg whites and pulse just to stir it in.

Whisk the vegetable mixture into the broth. Very slowly bring the mixture to a simmer over medium-low heat, stirring frequently but not vigorously just to keep the bottom of the pan clear. After about 20 to 30 minutes, when the egg mixture begins to cook and solidify then rise, stir less frequently. When the egg mixture has collected at the top of the broth, forming a raft, stop stirring and poke a 1-inch/2.5 cm vent hole through it. Reduce the heat to a bare simmer. Simmer for about 30 minutes as the raft solidifies further.

Line a fine-mesh strainer with several layers of cheesecloth. Gently push the raft out of the way and ladle the broth into the strainer. Pour the strained broth into a small saucepan. Season to taste with salt. Stir in the brandy and set aside.

Reheat just before serving.

The broth must be free of fat before it is clarified or pools of it will be visible in the final presentation. Chill it long enough and a solid disk will form that is very easy to remove completely rather than endlessly chasing it around the pot with a ladle. The egg white's proteins and the acid of the tomato form a glue-like web that captures all of the minuscule particles that normally cloud the broth.

Morel Mushroom Flans

Lightly oil 6 (½-cup/125 mL) ramekins or timbale molds. Preheat the oven to 325°F/160°C.

In a medium saucepan, gently sauté the shallots in the butter until softened. Add the garlic and sauté a minute more. Add the mushrooms, wine, and ½ cup/ 125 mL of the cream and bring to a simmer. Simmer until the mushrooms are fully hydrated (if using dried mushrooms) and the liquid has reduced by two-thirds.

Whisk together the remaining cream, eggs, and Parmesan. Stir in the mushroom-cream mixture and chives. Season to taste with salt and pepper. Divide the mixture evenly among the ramekins.

Place the ramekins in a pan large enough to hold them and pour simmering water two-thirds of the way up their sides. Bake for 30 minutes or until the custards are

2 shallots, minced

1 tablespoon / 15 mL butter

2 cloves garlic, minced

8 ounces / 250 g fresh or 1 cup / 250 mL dried morel or other mushrooms

½ cup / 125 mL Cabernet Sauvignon

1 ½ cups / 375 mL heavy cream

3 eggs

½ cup / 125 mL finely grated Parmesan cheese

¼ cup / 60 mL snipped chives

Salt and pepper

continued > >

just set. Remove the pan from the oven and let the custards sit in the water for 30 minutes. Serve immediately or refrigerate and reheat in the microwave. To serve, run a thin knife around the edge of the flans and turn out.

Removing the flans from their molds can be tricky; try fitting a small disk of lightly oiled wax paper into the bottom of the mold to help them release easier.

Arugula and Steak Julienne

Handful of arugula leaves

1 (6 to 8-ounce / 175 to 250 g) New York striploin

Stack the arugula leaves on top of each other and cut into very thin strips with a sharp knife. Trim any fat or sinew from the steak. Cut it into ⅛-inch/3 mm thick slices. Stack the slices and cut into ⅛-inch/3 mm julienne.

The Plate!

Chives

Turn out a mushroom flan into the center of each of 6 heated large, shallow bowls. Sprinkle the arugula chiffonade and steak julienne around each flan. Add ½ cup/ 125 mL or so of the hot consommé. Top each flan with 2 foie gras–stuffed morels and a flourish of chives. Serve with a drum roll!

> ◈ MORELS ◈
>
> *A harbinger of spring, this cousin of the truffle is one of the most luxurious members of the mushroom family. Its flavor is subtly reminiscent of earth, nuts, and smoke. The mushroom is hollow and can be easily stuffed. No one has been able to devise a method for cultivating morels, so they are only found in the wild. Mushroom hunters zealously guard the location of their prized patches.*

Whole Grain Country Bread
with Brown Butter, Olive Oil Butter,
Caramel Apple Butter, and Fazool

Bread reflects the respect a cook shows ingredients, and a baker's bread is a metaphor
for their kitchen aesthetic. This bread and its evolving maturity of flavors are a key part
of my menus. Simple to master, it will quickly show off your bake shop as well!

The spreads are all respectful of the bread they will accompany, each for a different dining occasion.

◇ 6 LARGE LOAVES ◇

TIMING: MAKE THE POOLISH FOR THE BREAD AT LEAST 12 AND PREFERABLY 24 HOURS IN ADVANCE.
| THE SPREADS MAY ALL BE MADE SEVERAL DAYS IN ADVANCE OR AS THE BREAD IS RISING AND BAKING.

Whole Grain Country Bread Poolish

Note: This bread recipe derives much of its flavor and character from the use of a fermented starter, the poolish. It is one of the keys to classic bread making.

Mix all the ingredients together in a large bowl. Cover and let ferment overnight, until the mixture is bubbly and almost doubles in volume.

Fermenting the starter overnight strengthens the yeast and boosts its flavor.

1 cup / 250 mL water

1 teaspoon / 5 mL active dry yeast

1 cup / 250 mL bread flour

½ cup / 125 mL whole wheat flour

½ cup / 125 mL light honey

Olive Oil Butter

Whip the butter until it is light and airy. Gradually whip in the olive oil until thoroughly combined.

¾ cup / 175 mL butter, at room temperature

¼ cup / 60 mL extra virgin olive oil

Brown Butter

¾ pound / 375 g butter (1 ½ cups / 375 mL), at room temperature

Place ¼ pound/125 g (½ cup/125 mL) of the butter in a small saucepan over medium heat and heat it until it melts and begins to foam. Continue heating it as the foam subsides and begins foaming a second time. Stir it gently. When the butter is golden brown and smells nutty, pour it into a metal container and cool to room temperature.

Whip the remaining butter until it is light and airy. Whip in the cooled brown butter until thoroughly combined.

Make sure you scrape all of the flavorful browned bits from the pan into the butter. If the temperatures are at room temperature the butters will whip and pipe easily.

Caramel Apple Butter

1 cup / 250 mL sugar

½ cup / 125 mL water

½ pound / 250 g butter (1 cup / 250 mL), cut in chunks

½ pound / 250 g apples, unpeeled, chopped (about 2 cups / 500 mL)

Place the sugar and water in a medium, heavy saucepan and heat it over medium heat until the ingredients melt together. Continue heating the mixture as the water evaporates and the melted sugar begins to caramelize.

When the caramel is a deep golden brown, add the remaining ingredients. Stir frequently and continue cooking until the apples are mushy, about 10 minutes.

Place the hot mixture in a blender and carefully purée until very smooth. Strain the mixture. Transfer to a storage container and refrigerate until chilled.

This is my favorite spread for breakfast. Don't stir the caramel! Patiently let it melt and when it begins to brown swirl the pan gently just to color the caramel evenly. Try different apple varieties and make a collection for tasting.

Whole Grain Country Bread

Note: The "mother" allows your bread to become more flavorful. If you make bread frequently, allow the mother to ferment in the refrigerator. It may also be frozen; thaw it for several days before use. Over time the cycle of use will add a great deal of character to your bread.

On a large clean, dry surface make a pile of the flours and salt. Mix them together briefly, then form a large well in the center, about 12 inches/30 cm in diameter.

Pour the water into the well and sprinkle the yeast over the water. Add the poolish and begin gradually blending the flours and liquids together with your fingers until all the flour is worked in.

Knead the dough for a few minutes, then add the mother from a previous batch of dough (if you have one), the 12-grain mix, and the sunflower seeds. Continue kneading until all of the ingredients are thoroughly incorporated; if necessary, sprinkle a little water over the dough to make it easier. Knead until the dough feels strong, smooth, and elastic, about 15 to 20 minutes.

Let the dough rest, covered, in a warm, dry place until it doubles in volume. Knock it down with your fist and cut it into 6 pieces. Reserve 1 pound/500 g of the dough for your next bread batch (the mother).

Roll up the dough pieces into tight balls. Arrange them on 2 lightly greased baking sheets, at least 6 inches/15 cm apart. Let them rest in a warm, dry place until they have doubled in volume.

Preheat the oven to 400°F/200°C. Bake the loaves until they are a deep golden brown and sound hollow when you tap them on the bottom. This will take 30 to 40 minutes.

8 cups / 2 L bread flour

3 cups / 750 mL whole wheat flour

2 tablespoons / 25 mL salt

3½ cups / 875 mL water

2 teaspoons / 10 mL active dry yeast

1 cup / 250 mL 12-grain or other whole grain mix

½ cup / 125 mL sunflower seeds

Fazool

1 cup / 250 mL dried white beans

½ cup / 125 mL chopped onion

¼ cup / 60 mL chopped carrot

1 tablespoon / 15 mL grated peeled ginger

2 cloves garlic, minced

2 cups / 500 mL water

½ cup / 125 mL extra virgin olive oil

¼ cup / 60 mL balsamic vinegar

Soak the beans overnight in enough water to cover. Drain the beans.

Place all the ingredients in a heavy saucepan, cover with a lid, and bring to a slow simmer. Simmer for 60 minutes, or until the water is absorbed and the beans and vegetables are soft. Stir frequently. If the pot is dry and the beans are not soft, add a little more water and continue cooking. If the mixture is soupy, remove the lid and cook longer until the water evaporates.

Purée until very smooth in a food processor. Refrigerate until ready to serve.

This spread is a great alternative for vegetarians and can also star at an afternoon cocktail party with the bread toasted.

The Plate!

Serve the bread warm and just sliced. Place the butters in decorative crocks or other small containers. Serve with a "come 'n get it!"

◇ WHEAT ◇

Whole wheat kernels, known as wheat berries, have three distinct parts. Bran is the fibrous outer coating. If sprouted, the germ is the future plant and is loaded with vitamins, minerals, and protein. The largest part, the endosperm, contains gluten. During the bread-making process, gluten forms an elastic web of long strands that trap the gas given off by the fermenting yeast, allowing the bread to rise.

Potato, Bacon, and Cheddar Tart
with Crème Fraîche and Spinach Salad

This spectacular showcase for a classic band of flavors will impress you in your own kitchen.
It's a show stopper when served whole and my favorite dish to bring to a party.
The elegant crème fraîche is simple to make and a luxurious sidekick for the tart.

◇ 8 SERVINGS ◇

TIMING: MAKE THE CRÈME FRAÎCHE THE DAY BEFORE. | MAKE THE TART AT LEAST 4 HOURS IN ADVANCE.
| SHORTLY BEFORE SERVING, MAKE THE SPINACH SALAD.

Crème Fraîche

Mix the cream and buttermilk together in a small bowl. Let the mixture rest in a covered canning jar at room temperature at least 12 hours or overnight, as it thickens. Chill it to thicken further.

1 cup / 250 mL heavy cream

1 tablespoon / 15 mL buttermilk

Add some of this crème fraîche to a new batch, eventually replacing the buttermilk as the yeast culture strengthens and gains its own distinct flavor.

Potato, Bacon, and Cheddar Tart

Preheat the oven to 325°F/160°C.

Line a 9-inch/23 cm cast-iron skillet with parchment paper. Trim the edges of the paper so it just clears the top edge of the pan. Spray the paper lightly with oil. Carefully arrange the bacon slices in a radial pattern from the center of the pan to the lower edge, then up and over the rim. Let the ends hang over the rim. Overlap the slices slightly around the sides of the pan; the bacon will be thicker in the pan's center. To reduce the thickness of the bacon in the center, stagger every other piece of bacon, starting it 2 inches/5 cm from the center and extending it farther

2 pounds / 1 kg bacon slices, at room temperature

Pepper

3 cups / 750 mL shredded sharp cheddar cheese

5 to 7 large baking potatoes (about 2½ to 3½ pounds / 1.25 to 1.75 kg)

Salt

1 cup / 250 mL minced onion

1 head garlic, peeled and minced

continued > >

than the adjacent slices. With the palm of your hand, flatten the center area, leaving no holes through the bacon. Grind some pepper onto the bacon, and sprinkle on 2 tablespoons/25 mL of the shredded cheddar.

Without peeling them, slice the potatoes thinly. The slices should be uniform, and about ¼ inch/5 mm thick. Arrange a circular layer of overlapping potato slices on top of the bacon around the edge of the skillet. Continue arranging rings of overlapping potato until the bottom of the pan is evenly covered. Sprinkle the potato with salt and pepper.

In a bowl, mix together the onion and garlic. Sprinkle some of the onion mixture onto the potato layer, then follow with a layer of the cheese. Cover with another layer of potato, pressing it down firmly before adding more seasoning. Repeat the layers until the potato reaches the top of the skillet. Add 2 more layers rising above the top of the pan, each inset 1 inch/2.5 cm from the previous layer. End with a layer of potato.

Taking 1 slice at a time, fold the bacon up and over the potato mound toward the center. Carefully overlap each slice, and repeat until the top is completely and neatly covered with bacon. Trim a small piece of parchment paper and place it in between a small ovenproof lid and the bacon. The lid is meant only to weigh the bacon ends down during the early stages of baking so they don't pull away and shrink. Don't use a large lid that will slow down the tart's baking time. Leave the lid on while the tart bakes.

Place the tart on a baking sheet, and put it in the oven. Bake it about 2½ to 3 hours. It is done when a thin knife inserted into it meets no resistance. The bacon will have browned and tightened, forming a crust, and the potatoes will have shrunk. Pour off any excess fat that is inside the pan. Let the tart stand for 30 minutes so that it will solidify.

If you can't find parchment paper, ask your favorite baker or restaurant waiter if you can have a sheet. Use the best, leanest bacon you can find — cheap bacon will shrink and tear. Let the bacon warm to room temperature before using it, so it will stretch slightly and be easier to work with. Use baking potatoes: their high starch content will help them adhere to each other as they bake. Other types will cause the tart to collapse.

Spinach Salad

Mix together the olive oil, red wine vinegar, mustard, and salt and pepper. Gently toss the spinach with the vinaigrette.

½ cup / 125 mL extra virgin olive oil

¼ cup / 60 mL red wine vinegar

2 tablespoons / 25 mL whole grain mustard

Salt and pepper to taste

8 ounces / 250 g clean, dry spinach leaves (about 6 cups / 1.5 L)

The Plate!

Place a pile of spinach salad on each of 8 plates. Reheat the tart slices in a microwave if needed, and place a slice of the tart on the salad. Top with a spoonful of the crème fraîche. Serve with a mmm!

◇ POTATO ◇

Today's potatoes are descendants of a wild root first cultivated by the Incas in South America. The average North American now consumes their weight in potatoes every year. Their delicate earthy flavor can be disturbed by the occasional green tinge shown in a potato exposed to light during its growth cycle. The pigment responsible is a bitter alkaloid, solanin. Cut out the affected part.

Roast Carrot and Goat Cheese Terrine
with a Salad of Savory Greens, Spicy Walnuts,
and Beet Vinaigrette

An all-vegetable presentation can be a masterpiece, highlighting the various flavors.
This plate strives for that mark, reaching it with attention to the details. I particularly like
the way the humble carrot steals the show!

 8 SERVINGS

TIMING: THE SPICY NUTS AND THE BEET VINAIGRETTE MAY BE MADE SEVERAL DAYS AHEAD. | MAKE THE TERRINE THE DAY BEFORE.
| PREPARE THE GREENS SEVERAL HOURS AHEAD.

Spicy Walnuts

1 egg white

½ cup / 125 mL brown sugar

1 tablespoon / 15 mL cinnamon

½ teaspoon / 2 mL salt

1 teaspoon / 5 mL Tabasco® pepper sauce

2½ cups / 625 mL walnut halves

Preheat the oven to 350°F/180°C.

In a stainless steel bowl whisk together the egg white, sugar, cinnamon, salt, and Tabasco® until the egg white increases in volume and the mixture thins slightly. Add the walnuts and toss them until they are evenly coated with the spice mixture.

Spread the walnuts evenly on a baking sheet and bake them for 12 to 15 minutes until they darken slightly and the crust bakes on. Don't burn them!

Let the nuts cool and store them in an airtight container at room temperature until needed.

The egg white serves as a glue that binds the spices and sugar to the nuts as they roast, building their flavors. Spread them out well or they will stick together.

Beet Vinaigrette

In a small saucepan, gently simmer the beets in the water until the beets are tender. Continue cooking until the water evaporates, leaving a glaze. Place the beets and glaze in a blender. Add the oil and vinegar and purée until very smooth. Season to taste with salt and pepper. Transfer to a squeeze bottle and refrigerate.

Be careful not to splash the beets on yourself—they are a strong dye. Adjust the consistency of the vinaigrette with water, if you like.

6 ounces / 175 g beets, chopped

1 cup / 250 mL water

½ cup / 125 mL extra virgin olive oil

¼ cup / 60 mL red wine vinegar

Salt and pepper

Roast Carrot and Goat Cheese Terrine

Note: Terrine molds are available in specialty kitchenware stores. A 12 by 4 by 3-inch/30 by 10 by 8 cm mold works best. A deep loaf pan or other similarly shaped molding vessel may be used.

Preheat the oven to 400°F/200°C. Lightly spray a terrine mold with vegetable oil spray. Line the mold with a layer of plastic wrap, smoothing out wrinkles and pressing out air bubbles.

Using a mandoline or a very sharp knife, slice the carrots lengthwise into ¼ inch/ 5 mm thick slices. Toss them with the olive oil and season with salt and pepper. Spread the carrots in a single layer on a baking sheet and roast until they are evenly browned and shriveling, about 30 minutes. It may be necessary to remove the carrots around the edge of the pan a few minutes before the others, as they will cook faster. Cool the carrots on the baking sheet.

5 pounds / 2.2 kg peeled carrots

1 cup / 250 mL extra virgin olive oil

Salt and pepper to taste

½ cup / 125 mL Chardonnay

2 envelopes unflavored gelatin

1½ pounds / 750 g goat cheese, at room temperature

1 cup / 250 mL snipped chives

continued >>

When the carrots are cooled make the terrine filling. Pour the wine into a small saucepan or stainless steel bowl and sprinkle with the gelatin. Wait 10 minutes for the gelatin to dissolve. Meanwhile, make the filling base.

Process the goat cheese and chives in a food processor until they are thoroughly mixed. The cheese should absorb the chives and turn pale green. Season with salt and pepper.

When the gelatin has dissolved, place the pan or bowl over or in simmering water. Stir briefly as the gelatin melts. After a few minutes, when the gelatin is a smooth liquid, pour it into the cheese mixture. Process briefly just to mix.

Line the bottom of the mold with carrot slices, trimming them as needed so they fit precisely. Add a few spoonfuls of the cheese mixture and spread a thin layer evenly over the carrots. Add another layer of carrots, pressing them into the cheese with an offset spatula to remove air spaces. Continue layering until the top of the mold is reached or the ingredients run out. Every layer or two, gently and firmly press the layers down with the spatula. Fold the plastic wrap over the terrine and refrigerate until firm, several hours or overnight.

When you are ready to serve the terrine, fold away the plastic wrap from the top and gently invert the mold onto a cutting board. Carefully remove the plastic. Slice the terrine with a sharp, thin knife or an electric knife.

Properly roasting the carrots deepens their flavor dramatically. Careful handling of the gelatin allows it to set like Jell-O, giving the terrine strength without detracting from its flavors. It must first be dissolved then melted for full strength. If the goat cheese is not at room temperature, the gelatin will set before you are done with the terrine.

Savory Greens

Soak the greens in room-temperature water for 15 minutes. Drain them and rinse them well in room-temperature water. Plunge the greens into ice water for 30 seconds, drain them again, and thoroughly dry them. Wrap the greens in a moist tea towel and store them, refrigerated, in a sealed container.

2 or 3 handfuls of a blend of tender savory greens such as tat soi, bok choy, nasturtium, spinach, and mâche

The greens are first fully hydrated in the room-temperature water — filling their cells — then crisped in the cold water. A greens spinner works best to dry them.

The Plate!

Squirt some of the beet vinaigrette onto each of 8 chilled salad plates. Toss the greens and the walnuts in ½ cup/125 mL of the vinaigrette and place a handful in the center of each plate. Top with a slice of the terrine and garnish with a nasturtium flower. Serve with a bzzzz!

Nasturtium flowers

> ### ◈ GOAT CHEESE ◈
>
> *There are many different types of goat cheese, or chèvre, each with individual characteristics. The most common is a soft, white creamy cheese with a fresh acidity and a distinct nutty goat flavor. The cheese is generally very young when consumed. As an apprentice cook I loathed the taste of it, but with experience came tolerance — now I am an avid fan and appreciate its bold flavors.*

Hazelnut-Crusted Roquefort Pudding with Seed Crisps and a Salad of Port-Glazed Figs, Frisee, and Cranberry Vinaigrette

Blue cheese fans of the world, unite! This is a great way to highlight a particularly good cheese with a palette of complementary flavors. Many of my guests prefer to end their meal on a note such as this.

◈ 6 SERVINGS ◈

TIMING: WHILE THE PUDDINGS ARE BAKING, MAKE THE CRISP DOUGH, GLAZED FIGS, AND CRANBERRY VINAIGRETTE.
| AT THE LAST MINUTE DRESS THE GREENS.

Hazelnut-Crusted Roquefort Pudding

1 cup / 250 mL hazelnuts

1 cup / 250 mL large-flake rolled oats

4 tablespoons / 60 mL butter, cut in pieces and frozen

½ cup / 125 mL cream cheese, at room temperature

12 ounces / 375 g Roquefort cheese

3 eggs

¼ cup / 60 mL snipped chives

Preheat the oven to 350°F/180°C.

Combine the nuts and oats in a food processor until they resemble coarse meal. Add the butter and process until the mixture forms a ball.

Divide the nut mixture among 6 ceramic ½-cup/125 mL ramekins. Pat it into place along the sides of the molds, forming an even, thin crust and paying close attention to the bottom corners. Make sure the crust is even and thin! Bake the crusts on a baking sheet for 15 minutes or until golden brown. Remove them from the oven and pat the nut crust sides into place once more. Do not turn the oven off.

Process the cheeses in a food processor until very smooth. Add the eggs and process just until they are completely mixed into the batter. Add the chives and pulse just to combine.

Carefully spoon the batter into the molds, avoiding the sides as they are very fragile and will break into the pudding.

Place the ramekins in a roasting pan and add enough boiling water to come almost all the way up the sides of the molds. Bake 30 to 40 minutes until the batter is set.

Let the puddings cool in the water for 30 minutes. Remove the molds from the water and carefully invert them onto your hand. Gently remove the puddings. Serve immediately or reserve.

The nut crust will eventually adhere to the blue cheese pudding but only in a thin, even layer. If the crust is uneven when you pat it in, much of it will remain in the mold. The only way to make a perfectly smooth batter is to have the cheese at room temperature. The water bath insulates the delicate puddings from the direct heat of the oven. The puddings may be removed from their molds and refrigerated, then reheated in a microwave.

Seed Crisps

Preheat the oven to 325°F/160°C. Line a baking sheet with a silicone baking mat or parchment paper.

Melt the butter, sugar, corn syrup, and cream in a small saucepan over medium-low heat, stirring. Remove from the heat and stir in the seeds until thoroughly combined. Transfer to a small bowl and refrigerate until hardened.

Form the dough into at least 20 (½-teaspoon/2 mL) balls and place 4 inches/10 cm apart on the baking sheet. Bake for 8 to 10 minutes until toasted. Begin loosening them from the mat as they cool completely. As soon as possible cut each circle in half with the edge of a thin spatula. They are very fragile.

Store in an airtight container.

4 tablespoons / 60 mL butter

¼ cup / 60 mL sugar

2 tablespoons / 25 mL corn syrup

2 tablespoons / 25 mL heavy cream

½ cup / 125 mL sesame seeds

¼ cup / 60 mL poppy seeds

For a spontaneous napoleon, bake the batter in bigger disks and layer fruits with them. They are fragile, so make more than you need in case some break.

Port-Glazed Figs

½ cup / 125 mL honey

½ cup / 125 mL good-quality Tawny Port

6 fresh figs

In a saucepan, bring the honey and port to a simmer, stirring, and reduce by half. Meanwhile quarter the figs. Poach them briefly in the syrup, just long enough for them to heat through and absorb the syrup. Place them on a piece of parchment paper and refrigerate. Reserve the poaching syrup.

If you are using dry figs, simmer them longer so they can rehydrate a bit.

Cranberry Vinaigrette

½ cup / 125 mL cranberries

¼ cup / 60 mL red wine vinegar

2 tablespoons / 25 mL honey

1 teaspoon / 5 mL Tabasco® pepper sauce

4 tablespoons / 60 mL extra virgin olive oil

Place the berries, vinegar, honey, and Tabasco® in a small saucepan. Bring them to a simmer and continue simmering a few minutes more as the cranberries soften. Pour the mixture into a blender, add the olive oil, and purée. Pour the vinaigrette into a squeeze bottle and reserve.

Dried, fresh, or frozen berries work equally well in this recipe.

The Plate!

Several handfuls of salad greens, cleaned well and dried thoroughly

Salt and pepper

Toss the greens with enough vinaigrette to lightly coat them. Toss them with salt and pepper to taste. Place a small pile of the greens in the center of each of 6 cold salad plates. Garnish the plates with some of the vinaigrette. Place a warm pudding on the greens and top with a fig and some crisps. Drip some of the fig poaching syrup on the plate. Serve with a cheesy grin!

Oyster Mushroom Strudel
with Spinach Sauce and a Merlot Swirl

Strudels are not just for dessert! This one is the perfect way to spotlight
your favorite mushroom within an all-vegetable presentation.

◇ 6 SERVINGS ◇

TIMING: MAKE THE TWO SAUCES WHILE THE STRUDEL IS BAKING. | THE SPINACH SAUCE MAY ALSO BE MADE THE DAY BEFORE.

Oyster Mushroom Strudel

Preheat the oven to 375°F/190°C.

Reserve some mushrooms for garnish. Thinly slice the remaining mushroom stems and roughly chop the heads.

Melt 1 tablespoon/15 mL of the butter in a large nonstick sauté pan. Add one-quarter of the onions and sauté for a few minutes until golden. Add one-quarter of the garlic and one-quarter of the mushrooms, and season with salt and pepper. Continue sautéing until the mushrooms begin to brown. Repeat with the remaining butter, onion, garlic, and mushrooms. Use more butter if necessary.

When all the mushrooms are done, finely chop half of the mixture in a food processor. In a large bowl, mix together the chopped mushrooms, the remaining mushrooms, the sage leaves, and Parmesan.

Keep the phyllo dough covered with a barely moist towel while working with each sheet. Lay the first sheet of the phyllo dough on a clean, dry surface and brush with clarified butter. Layer on a second sheet, butter it, and sprinkle with the bread crumbs. Lightly season with salt and pepper. Add the third sheet, butter it, and top with the fourth sheet. If necessary use more clarified butter or vegetable oil to brush the sheets.

3 pounds / 1.5 kg oyster mushrooms or other specialty mushroom

4 tablespoons / 60 mL butter

1 large onion, minced

1 tablespoon / 15 mL minced garlic

Salt and pepper to taste

¼ cup / 60 mL sliced sage leaves

1 cup / 250 mL grated Parmesan cheese

4 sheets phyllo dough

1 tablespoon / 15 mL clarified butter

¼ cup / 60 mL dried bread crumbs

continued >>

Form an even log-shaped mound of the mushroom mixture along a longer edge of the dough, leaving a 1-inch/2.5 cm border. Make sure the filling extends to the edge of the pastry at each end. Brush the pastry with more clarified butter and then carefully roll the filling up tightly into the pastry. If any mixture falls out the ends, push it back in. Brush the pastry with more clarified butter. Make a series of shallow cuts with a serrated knife into the top of the strudel to mark the desired portions.

Place in a baguette mold or on a double baking sheet and bake for 30 to 45 minutes until the pastry is golden brown and the filling is heated through.

The cooking method is designed to extract water from the mushrooms before they are wrapped in phyllo pastry. The water would otherwise make the phyllo soggy. The towel should be just moist enough for its fibers to swell and keep air from drying out the phyllo dough. Try adding other dry cheeses to the mushroom mixture for a different flavor. The cuts on the strudel give steam a chance to vent so it doesn't split the pastry.

Spinach Sauce

1 tablespoon / 15 mL butter

½ cup / 125 mL minced onion

2 large cloves garlic, minced

1 (10 ounce / 284 g) package spinach, cleaned

½ cup / 125 mL water

Salt and pepper

Melt the butter in a heavy saucepan. Add the onion and sauté briefly until soft. Add the garlic and sauté for 1 minute.

Add the spinach leaves and water, then stir quickly until the spinach has wilted.

Purée the mixture thoroughly in a blender. Make sure the vent hole is left open so that the hot liquid doesn't expand violently; loosely cover the top with a kitchen towel to contain splatters.

Season with salt and pepper to taste.

Serve the sauce immediately or chill it rapidly in an ice bath. It will last a day in the refrigerator if you place a piece of plastic wrap directly on the surface of the sauce. Reheat it before serving.

The stems of the spinach can be tough and fibrous and clog the blender. Don't overcook the spinach or its color will be drab, and for the best color serve the sauce immediately.

Merlot Swirl

Pour the Merlot into a saucepan and bring to a simmer over medium heat. Reduce it until it is thick and syrupy, then stir in the cream.

Simmer the mixture gently until it has reduced to about ¼ cup/60 mL and thickened.

If the sauce "breaks" just whisk it back together with a few drops of cream.

2 cups / 500 mL Merlot
½ cup / 125 mL heavy cream

The Plate!

Reheat the spinach sauce if needed. Pour ¼ cup/60 mL in the center of each of 6 hot plates. Spoon some of the Merlot swirl onto the spinach sauce. Swirl it gently by smoothly shaking the plate.

Quickly sauté the mushrooms in the butter just to heat them through. Arrange a few sautéed oyster mushrooms on the sauces. Place a slice of the strudel on the mushrooms and garnish with a sprig of sage. Serve with a fanfare!

Reserved oyster mushrooms
1 tablespoon / 15 mL butter
Sage sprigs

Smoked Salmon and Dill Roulade
with Whole-Wheat Pancakes, Salmon Caviar, and Dandelion Greens Salad

Smoked salmon can be wonderful served plain with some of the ingredients in this presentation.
But when combined like this, the salmon is given a starring role in a classy show.
Make sure you use awesome smoked salmon!

◇ 6 SERVINGS ◇

TIMING: MAKE THE SALAD DRESSING THE DAY BEFORE. | MAKE THE ROULADE AT LEAST A DAY BEFORE; IT MAY ALSO BE FROZEN.
| MAKE THE PANCAKE BATTER 1 HOUR AHEAD, AND MAKE THE PANCAKES SHORTLY BEFORE SERVING.

Smoked Salmon and Dill Roulade

1 side unsliced smoked salmon

8 ounces / 250 g soft cream cheese

½ cup / 125 mL snipped dill

2 tablespoons / 25 mL dry vermouth

Salt and pepper to taste

Lay a piece of plastic wrap on a moistened surface. Trim the irregular ends and thinner belly section off of the salmon and reserve for the mousse. Thinly slice the remaining salmon across its top and lay it on the plastic wrap, forming a rectangle about 6 by 4 inches/15 by 10 cm. Reserve the remaining salmon for another use.

Place the cream cheese, reserved salmon scraps, dill, vermouth, and salt and pepper in a food processor and process until smooth. Stop the machine after a few moments and wipe down the sides with a rubber spatula.

Spread the mousse evenly over the smoked salmon. Using the plastic wrap as a guide, and starting from a long end, roll the salmon up into a log. Peel back the plastic wrap as you go so that it doesn't get rolled into the roulade. Wrap the salmon in the plastic, grasp the ends, and twirl the roulade, tightening the plastic and forcing the roulade into a perfect round shape.

Refrigerate until solid, at least 60 minutes.

Save time by spreading the filling onto the pancakes and adding the sliced salmon. In that case the filling is best served at room temperature.

Dandelion Greens Salad

Whisk together all the ingredients except the greens. Let the vinaigrette rest at least 60 minutes and preferably overnight. Stir it well before use.

When ready to serve, toss the greens in the vinaigrette.

I pick the greens for this salad from the front yard while they are still young and tender and measure no more than 4 inches long (otherwise they are too bitter). Make sure you haven't used chemicals on them, and wash them well.

Minced zest and juice of 2 lemons

½ cup / 125 mL extra virgin olive oil

1 tablespoon / 15 mL capers, minced

2 tablespoons / 25 mL minced red onion

2 tablespoons / 25 mL honey

Several handfuls of small, tender dandelion greens

Whole-Wheat Pancakes

Thoroughly mix together all the dry ingredients in a medium bowl. In a separate bowl, lightly beat the eggs. Whisk in the melted butter. Stir in the milk until completely blended.

Add the wet ingredients to the dry ingredients and stir with a spoon until just combined; leave the batter slightly lumpy. Let it rest for 60 minutes.

Heat a sauté pan or skillet over a medium-high heat, and melt 1 tablespoon/ 15 mL of butter. Spoon 1 tablespoon/15 mL of batter per pancake into the pan. Turn the pancakes when the bottom is golden brown. Try to make pancakes only slightly bigger than the roulade's diameter. Continue making the pancakes until the batter is used up; make at least 18. Keep the pancakes warm for up to 30 minutes between folds of a moistened towel in a warm oven.

The pan is hot enough when water droplets dance on its surface instead of slowly simmering or instantly evaporating.

1 cup / 250 mL whole wheat flour

½ cup / 125 mL all-purpose flour

1 ½ teaspoons / 7 mL baking powder

1 teaspoon / 5 mL salt

2 eggs

3 tablespoons / 45 mL butter, melted

1 ½ cups / 375 mL milk

Additional butter for frying pancakes

The Plate!

Salmon caviar

Dill sprigs

Lemon zest

Unwrap the roulade and thinly slice it. Make a napoleon by placing one slice of roulade on a pancake. Top with another pancake, another slice of roulade, and a third pancake. Make 5 more napoleons. Arrange the dressed greens on 6 plates and top with a napoleon. Place a dollop of salmon caviar on top of each napoleon, garnish with a dill sprig, and sprinkle some lemon zest around the plate. Serve with a "bon appétit!"

> ### ❖ SMOKED SALMON ❖
>
> *Salmon's overwhelming availability to native peoples inspired numerous necessary preserving methods. Today the methods survive as a form of edible art. The best are lightly cured with salt and sometimes sugar or spices, then smoked with a distinct hardwood. The process doesn't heat the salmon, so it retains a rich texture. At home I cure my fillets with coarse sea salt, brown sugar, and cinnamon, then cold-smoke them in an old refrigerator with maple chips!*

Sandwich of Thousand-Layer Pastry, Roast Lobster, and Aïoli with Blood Orange Relish

The multitude of layers in the puff pastry inspire this fancy dressed-up sandwich. The flavors remind me of a picnic, but it's best served in the dining room. The accompanying aïoli is the single best way I know of to show off the wild pungency and bite of garlic.

◇ 4 SERVINGS ◇

TIMING: MAKE THE AÏOLI SEVERAL DAYS AHEAD. | BAKE THE SANDWICH PASTRY THE DAY BEFORE. | MAKE THE RELISH WHILE THE LOBSTER IS ROASTING.

Aïoli

Place the yolks, lemon zest, and garlic in a small food processor. Purée until smooth.

With the motor running, add the oil a few drops at a time. Begin slowly but add a little faster as the sauce begins to thicken and stiffen. Make sure that the oil is fully incorporated before adding more. Add the lemon juice and mix until smooth. Season with salt and pepper. Refrigerate the sauce in a squeeze bottle or jar for as long as several days before needed.

The raw egg yolks serve as an emulsifier, allowing the oil and juice mixture to blend properly. Use the freshest eggs and there's no risk of salmonella.

2 egg yolks

Zest and juice of 2 lemons

6 cloves garlic

1 cup / 250 mL extra virgin olive oil

Salt and pepper to taste

Thousand-Layer Sandwich Pastry

Preheat the oven to 400°F/200°C. Lightly oil a baking sheet or line it with parchment paper.

1 package puff pastry dough, thawed

2 tablespoons / 25 mL butter, melted

continued > >

On a lightly floured surface, roll out the dough into an 8 by 9-inch / 20 by 23 cm rectangle; let rest. Using a very sharp knife, slice the rectangle into 3 by 2-inch / 8 by 5 cm rectangles. Don't crush the layers together at the edges of the rectangles. Place the rectangles on the baking sheet. Brush them lightly with the melted butter.

Bake for 10 to 15 minutes until golden brown and puffy. Let cool on a rack and store in an airtight container.

Use a double-bottomed baking pan placed in the center of the oven so the pastry doesn't burn.

Roast Lobster

4 tablespoons / 60 mL butter, at room temperature

2 tablespoons / 25 mL minced garlic

Salt and pepper to taste

2 (1 ½ to 2-pound / 750 g to 1 kg) live female lobsters

Preheat the oven to 450°F/230°C. Whisk together the butter, garlic, salt and pepper.

Cut the live lobster in half from tail to head, leaving the claws attached. Remove and discard the head sac and rinse out the head of the lobster. Leave any liver (pale green) or roe (bright red or dark green egg sac) intact. Brush the meat with butter and place lobsters on a baking pan. Roast for 10 minutes.

When the tail and knuckle meat is cool enough to handle, remove it and coarsely chop it with any roe or liver. Reserve the meat. Carefully remove the claw meat without damaging it. First, gently loosen and remove the smaller movable pincer. Then cut into the base of the claw shell, cracking it off and exposing the base of the claw meat. Pull out the claw, then remove the internal cartilage if it didn't already come out. Reserve the claw meat whole.

Steamed or canned lobster may be substituted. Make sure the lobster roe and liver are fully cooked before using. Sometimes they require a moment in the microwave just to finish them.

Island Blue Mussel and Sweet Potato Chowder
with Bay Fortune Spiced Bread Sticks,
Spicy Butter, and a Stuffed Onion
(page 40)

Whole Grain Country Bread with Brown Butter,
Olive Oil Butter, Caramel Apple Butter, and Fazool
(page 51)

Potato, Bacon, and Cheddar Tart
with Crème Fraîche and Spinach Salad
(page 55)

Roast Carrot and Goat Cheese Terrine
with a Salad of Savory Greens, Spicy Walnuts,
and Beet Vinaigrette
(page 58)

Blood Orange Relish

With a sharp knife remove the peel and outer membrane from the oranges. Working over a bowl to catch the juices, section the oranges. Place the juice in a small saucepan and reduce to a syrup over medium heat. Swirl in the butter and set aside.

Meanwhile, toss the remaining ingredients together in a bowl just to combine them.

You may substitute other oranges if blood oranges are unavailable. Try to keep the orange sections whole as you cut them out using the internal membranes as guidelines for your very sharp paring knife. And remember to take out the seeds!

4 blood oranges

1 tablespoon / 15 mL butter

2 tablespoons / 25 mL finely sliced mint leaves

2 tablespoons / 25 mL finely minced red onion

1 tablespoon / 15 mL capers

1 tablespoon / 15 mL extra virgin olive oil

Salt and pepper to taste

The Plate!

Fold together the chopped lobster and ¼ cup/60 mL of the aïoli. Layer the lobster onto 8 of the pastry rectangles with a few sorrel leaves. Form 4 stacks with these and top with the remaining 4 rectangles. Place the remaining aïoli in a squeeze bottle and pipe onto 4 plates in a decorative pattern. Place a sandwich in the center of each plate. Top with some of the orange relish and drizzle some of the blood orange reduction onto each plate. Serve with a jump!

Sorrel leaves or other savory greens

❖ BLOOD ORANGES ❖

As a young apprentice cook getting his feet wet in the great big world of cuisine, I saw many new things. The first ingredient I encountered that I had never even imagined before was a blood orange. It jolted me awake with its vibrant color and flavor, and I began to sense the amazing presence an ingredient can bear in cooking. Imagine a crimson red fruit with a bolder orange flavor than its pale cousins. I owe a debt to this gorgeous fruit!

Cinnamon Sweetbread and Pine Nut Crisp Stack with Warm Carrot Olive Oil Emulsion, Basil Coulis, and Balsamic Vinegar Glazed Carrots

Sweetbreads, the thymus glands of young calves, are an entry-level specialty meat. They have a very mild, delicate flavor and a wonderful texture that combines easily with the flavors of this presentation. The richness of the carrot sauce and the hearty pine nut flavors are particularly alluring in tandem with the cool basil.

◇ 4 SERVINGS ◇

TIMING: THE PINE NUT CRISP BATTER, BASIL COULIS, CARROT JUICE REDUCTION, FRIED BASIL LEAVES, AND POACHED SWEETBREADS MAY ALL BE MADE AHEAD. | AN HOUR OR TWO BEFORE SERVING MAKE THE PINE NUT CRISPS. | START THE CARROTS 30 MINUTES BEFORE SERVING. FRY THE SWEETBREADS AT THE LAST MINUTE.

Pine Nut Crisps

2 tablespoons / 25 mL butter

2 tablespoons / 25 mL brown sugar

1 egg

1 cup / 250 mL pine nuts

½ cup / 125 mL grated excellent Parmesan cheese

Salt

Cream the butter and sugar together in a food processor. Add the egg and mix in. Add half of the nuts, the cheese, and a pinch of salt and mix just until smooth. Stir in the remaining nuts by hand. Refrigerate the batter until chilled.

Preheat the oven to 350°F/180°C. Lightly oil a baking sheet or line it with a nonstick baking mat or parchment paper. Cut a 3-inch/8 cm circle out of a food-safe plastic lid. Lay the template on the baking sheet and spread 1 heaping tablespoon/15 mL of batter through it. Alternatively, place a small spoonful of the batter on the baking sheet and press it with the back of a spatula into an even layer about 3 inches/8 cm wide.

Bake the crisps until golden brown and crisp, about 10 to 12 minutes, turning the tray once. Let them cool on a rack. Repeat until you have 12 crisps. Store them in an airtight container.

This recipe is designed to make just enough batter needed to hold the pine nuts together. Make sure the nuts are in one even layer so they bake evenly in the crisps.

Basil Coulis

In a blender or small food processor, purée the basil and oil until very smooth. Taste and season. Reserve in a squeeze bottle until needed.

1 cup / 250 mL packed basil leaves

¼ cup / 60 mL extra virgin olive oil

Salt and pepper to taste

Warm Carrot Olive Emulsion

Place the carrot juice, lemon juice and zest, star anise, cinnamon, and chili flakes in a small saucepan and reduce, over medium heat, to ½ cup/125 mL. Strain the juice and discard the solids. Season to taste with salt, and set aside.

Just before serving, reheat the carrot juice. Add the olive oil and whip the broth to a froth with an immersion blender or whisk. Serve immediately.

You can use a blender to make this sauce but an immersion blender is much easier to clean. Big, woody carrots have the most flavorful juice. Small, young ones are pale in comparison.

4 cups / 1 L fresh carrot juice

Zest and juice of 1 lemon

2 whole star anise

½ teaspoon / 2 mL cinnamon

Pinch of dried chili flakes

Salt

4 tablespoons / 60 mL extra virgin olive oil

Fried Basil Leaves

Using a countertop deep-fryer and following the manufacturer's instructions, fry the basil leaves just until crisp. (Alternatively, fill a large, heavy saucepan with 2 inches/5 cm of oil. Heat the oil to 365°F/185°C and fry the leaves briefly, just until crisp.) Drain them on paper towels and reserve in an airtight container.

12 large or 24 small basil leaves

Cinnamon Sweetbreads

1 pound / 500 g sweetbreads

Juice of 1 lemon

1 onion, sliced

4 cloves garlic, smashed

2 bay leaves

1 cup / 250 mL semolina flour

1 tablespoon / 15 mL cinnamon

½ cup / 125 mL olive oil

Salt and pepper to taste

Place the sweetbreads in a medium saucepan and cover them with cold water. Add the lemon juice, onion, garlic, and bay leaves, and bring to a boil over medium heat. Reduce heat and simmer for 5 more minutes. Gently drain them in a strainer basket, then plunge the basket into ice water. Drain once more, and lay them on paper towels. Gently pull away any membrane or other matter. Refrigerate, covered, until firm. (The sweetbreads may be prepared to this point up to 1 day ahead.)

Shortly before serving, cut the sweetbreads into ½-inch/ 1 cm thick slices. Mix the flour and cinnamon together and toss the sweetbreads in the mixture until they are uniformly coated.

Heat the oil in a medium nonstick sauté pan over medium-high heat. Add the sweetbreads and brown them perfectly on both sides. Season, then drain briefly on paper towels. Serve immediately.

You may substitute plain flour for the semolina. Cut the sweetbreads into even, thin slices so there is more surface area to brown, adding flavor.

Balsamic Glazed Carrots

1 pound / 500 g carrots , cut into 3 by ½ by ½-inch / 8 by 1 by 1 cm sticks

4 tablespoons / 60 mL olive oil

Salt and pepper to taste

2 tablespoons / 25 mL the best balsamic vinegar you can find and afford

Preheat the oven to 400°F/200°C.

In a roasting pan, toss the carrots with the oil and salt and pepper. Roast the carrots for 10 minutes, then shake the pan. Roast the carrots until caramelized, another 20 minutes, stirring them frequently.

Transfer the carrots to a bowl. Scrape the remaining bits and oil from the pan into the carrots. Add the vinegar and toss until the carrots are evenly coated. Reserve briefly or serve immediately.

Real balsamic vinegar is hard to find and very valuable. A good substitute is to reduce common balsamic vinegar by two-thirds, intensifying its flavors.

The Plate!

Pour about ¼ cup/60 mL of the warm carrot emulsion into each of 4 warm large, shallow bowls. Position a small tight pile of the glazed carrots in the center of the bowl. Place a nut crisp level on the carrots. Arrange several slices of sweetbread and a fried basil leaf or two on the crisp. Add another crisp and repeat. Top with the last crisp. Decorate with the basil coulis and top with a fresh basil sprig. Serve with a flash!

Basil sprigs

◈ BALSAMIC VINEGAR ◈

Authentic balsamic vinegar is a carefully crafted, tightly controlled Italian specialty. It is made from fresh grape juices concentrated through years of evaporation through a series of wooden barrels. The resulting liqueur-like vinegar is intensely flavorful, rarely heated, and very expensive. Its cheaper commercial pretenders are merely thin wine vinegar with caramel cooked in. Simmer and reduce them to approximate the real thing. For an absolute gastronomic experience sprinkle a few drops of the real thing on a ball of premium vanilla ice cream.

Olive Oil–Seared Tuna
with Tomato Anchovy Sauce,
Lemon Basil Pistou, and Saffron Ratatouille

Tuna is the beef of the deep, and its rich hearty flavors benefit from the same cooking treatment its landlubber cousin receives. Like great meat it is best served rare, as it dries out quickly, losing its natural essence. The flavors of the Mediterranean are a natural accompaniment for its unctuousness.

◇ 6 SERVINGS, WITH LEFTOVERS ◇

TIMING: MAKE THE RATATOUILLE AND THE PISTOU AND REFRIGERATE OVERNIGHT. | MAKE THE ANCHOVY SAUCE.
| BRING A POT OF SALTED WATER TO THE BOIL FOR SCALDING THE CHARD. | COOK THE TUNA AS YOU BEGIN THE PRESENTATION STEPS.

Saffron Ratatouille

1 cup / 250 mL minced onion

3 tablespoons / 45 mL extra virgin olive oil

4 cloves garlic, minced

1 cup / 250 mL chopped tomato

1 teaspoon / 5 mL minced jalapeño

½ teaspoon / 2 mL saffron threads

1 cup / 250 mL chopped eggplant

1 cup / 250 mL chopped green pepper

1 cup / 250 mL chopped zucchini

1 teaspoon / 5 mL salt

In a medium saucepan, cook the onion in 1 tablespoon/15 mL of the oil until golden brown. Add the garlic and continue cooking for several minutes more. Add the tomato, jalapeño, and saffron. Turn the heat to low, and continue cooking until much of the liquid has evaporated, about 15 minutes.

While the tomato mixture is simmering, heat 1 tablespoon/15 mL of the remaining oil in a nonstick sauté pan over high heat. Add the eggplant and sauté until it is just cooked through. Place the eggplant in a large bowl and set aside. Sauté the green pepper in ½ tablespoon/7 mL of the remaining oil until brightly colored and just cooked through. Place the green pepper in the bowl with the eggplant. Follow the same procedure to cook the zucchini to the same degree of doneness, and add the zucchini to the eggplant and green pepper.

Pour the tomato mixture over the eggplant, green pepper, and zucchini. Add the salt and toss the mixture until completely mixed. Refrigerate overnight.

By cooking the vegetables separately, you don't end up with a dull-looking, plain-tasting stew. Don't use pale, lifeless supermarket tomatoes: if you can't find fresh vine-ripened tomatoes, use canned tomatoes.

Lemon Basil Pistou

Place all the ingredients in a food processor and process until smooth. Reserve the pistou until needed. It may be made 1 day in advance and refrigerated, covered, until needed.

You may use a blender or, for an authentic touch, try a mortar and pestle to make this pistou.

4 cups / 1 L basil sprigs

Zest and juice of 1 lemon

½ teaspoon / 2 mL salt

½ cup / 125 mL extra virgin olive oil

½ cup / 125 mL grated good-quality Parmesan cheese

½ teaspoon / 2 mL Tabasco® pepper sauce

Tomato Anchovy Sauce

Reserve 1 tablespoon/15 mL of the lemon juice for another use. Combine the remaining lemon juice, lemon zest, tomato, anchovies, oil, and Tabasco® in a blender and process until very smooth.

Strain the sauce through a fine-mesh strainer. Set aside. Heat it just before serving.

Depending on the brininess of the anchovies, it may be necessary to add a pinch of salt to balance the sauce.

Zest and juice of 2 lemons

2 medium tomatoes, puréed (about 1 cup / 250 mL)

8 anchovies, oil or brine squeezed out*

4 tablespoons / 60 mL extra virgin olive oil

½ teaspoon / 2 mL Tabasco® pepper sauce

*USE SALT CURED ANCHOVIES IF AVAILABLE. THEY ARE OF HIGHER QUALITY.

Olive Oil–Seared Tuna

Coarsely grind the pepper onto both sides of the tuna steaks. Heat a large cast-iron skillet over high heat for several minutes. Add the oil and heat it until it just begins to smoke. Add the tuna steaks. Sear on one side for 2 to 3 minutes until crisp, then turn the steaks over and sear the other side. (Begin the presentation as you are cooking the tuna.) Let the fish rest briefly before serving.   continued > >

6 (4 to 6-ounce / 125 to 175 g) tuna fillets, each 2 inches / 15 cm thick

Pepper

4 tablespoons / 60 mL extra virgin olive oil

The Plate!

6 large Swiss chard leaves

Basil sprigs

Salt

Reheat the ratatouille in a microwave or in a saucepan on medium heat. Reheat the tomato anchovy sauce. Meanwhile, bring a pot of salted water to the boil. Dip each chard leaf into the boiling water briefly, just long enough to wilt the leaf. Fit the leaf into a 4-inch/10 cm wide circular mold about 1 inch/2.5 cm tall. Fill the leaf-lined mold with ratatouille. Fold the ends of the leaf over at the top to seal it. Using a wide spatula, invert the filled mold onto a warm dinner plate. Carefully remove the mold by gently lifting it directly up. Repeat for each plate.

Pour the sauce onto each plate in 3 places, framing the ratatouille. Cut each tuna steak into 3 pieces, and arrange them around the plate. Season the tuna with salt. Top the tuna with a spoonful of the pistou and drizzle some of the pistou onto the tomato sauce. Garnish with a basil sprig. Serve with a splash!

◇ TUNA ◇

Tuna must swim at an average speed of 25 to 30 mph, 24 hours a day, with no rest ever, to pass an adequate supply of oxygen-rich seawater over their gills. The head of the large tuna family is the bluefin, which can weigh more than a large steer. Its deep red flesh is strongly flavored and a favorite of sushi fans, but too strong for most palates. My favorite is the ahi, while canners prefer the albacore, skipjack, and yellowfin varieties.

She Lobster with Roast Corn Pudding, Smoked Clam Corn Chowder, Pea Shoots, and Red Pepper Relish

The sweetness of lobster makes it a willing participant in this bright group of crisp flavors. The female's rich roe and liver add a sophisticated depth of flavor often missing from lobster dishes. A few southwestern hints complete the eclectic balance of the presentation.

◇ 6 SERVINGS ◇

TIMING: MAKE THE RED PEPPER RELISH AHEAD. │ SMOKE THE CLAMS FOR THE CHOWDER 2 DAYS BEFORE.
│ MAKE THE CHOWDER THE DAY BEFORE. │ MAKE THE PUDDING THE DAY BEFORE OR SEVERAL HOURS BEFORE.

Red Pepper Relish

Place all the ingredients in a small saucepan and bring them to a simmer. Simmer for about 20 minutes as it reduces and forms a syrupy relish. Store in the refrigerator. Let the relish come to room temperature before serving.

This relish is great with grilled meat and chicken and will last a long time in the refrigerator. Try adding your favorite herbs or spices to customize it.

1 red pepper, diced

1 red onion, diced

Zest and juice of 4 limes

2 tablespoons / 25 mL honey

¼ teaspoon / 1 mL salt

1 tablespoon / 15 mL green jalapeño Tabasco® pepper sauce

2 tablespoons / 25 mL extra virgin olive oil

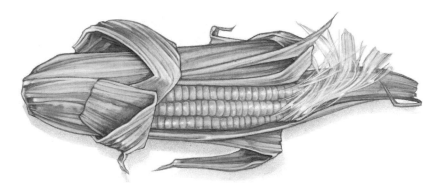

Smoked Clam Corn Chowder

1 cup / 250 mL whole clams

4 ears corn

6 cups / 1.5 L milk

4 tablespoons / 60 mL butter

1 large onion, chopped

2 cloves garlic, minced

1 stalk celery, chopped

1 teaspoon / 5 mL salt

Pepper to taste

Smoke the clams: Using 2 metal pans of equal size or a wok, make a stovetop smoker. Fill the bottom of one pan or the wok with hardwood chips. Place a screen over the pan. Invert the second pan or the wok top over the rack, creating a smoking chamber. Place the smoker over medium heat until the wood chips begin to smoke. Place the clams on the screen and smoke for 5 minutes. Make sure you have good ventilation or do this outdoors, as it will generate a *lot* of smoke. Let the clams rest, refrigerated, for 24 hours.

Cut the kernels off the corn ears. Break the cobs into 3 pieces and place in a stockpot. Cover with the milk and bring to the boil. Reduce the heat to a simmer and continue cooking for 30 to 60 minutes, infusing the milk with the corn flavor. The broth will reduce slightly along the way. (The corn cobs for the roast corn pudding may be simmered along with these corn cobs; double the amount of milk.) Reserve the corn kernels from the cobs.

In a large, heavy saucepan, melt the butter. Add the onions, garlic, and celery and sauté briefly until slightly softened. Add 4 cups/1 L of the corn cob broth; if there's not enough, add enough milk to measure 4 cups/1 L. Add the reserved corn and smoked clams and bring the chowder to a simmer. Season with the salt and pepper. Simmer for 30 minutes. Let the chowder rest for 24 hours; the flavor will improve overnight.

Gently reheat the chowder just before serving.

Look for smoked clams in a specialty food store. You may also skip the smoking step. Like all chowders, an overnight rest gives the flavors a chance to blend and harmonize.

Lobster

Bring several inches of water to a rolling boil in a large pot with a tight-fitting lid. Place the lobsters in the pot, replace the lid, and let steam for 5 to 7 minutes until the lobsters have turned red all over. Remove the claws and knuckles from the lobsters and return to the pot. Cook them for an additional 3 minutes.

Cut the tails in half lengthwise and remove the two tail meat sections, reserving any liver (pale green) or roe (bright red or dark green egg sac). The tails will not be fully cooked at this point. Set aside the tail meat.

Remove any remaining liver or roe from the head section and reserve for the corn pudding. Reserve the antennas.

Separate the claws from the knuckles. Carefully remove the claw meat without damaging it. First, gently loosen and remove the smaller movable pincer. Then cut into the base of the claw shell, cracking it off and exposing the base of the claw meat. Pull out the claw, then remove the internal cartilage if it didn't already come out. Reserve the meat, covered and refrigerated.

Remove the knuckle meat by cutting open the shell and taking out the meat inside. Reserve for the corn pudding.

Just before serving, melt the butter in a nonstick skillet over medium-high heat. Add the tail and claw meat and sauté just to heat through. Season the lobster lightly with salt and pepper. Pour in the wine and stir. Allow it to reduce quickly, glazing the lobster.

6 (1 ½-pound / 750 g) live female lobsters

4 tablespoons / 60 mL butter

Salt and pepper to taste

½ cup / 125 mL white wine

Because the claws' shells are thicker they require a longer cooking time. If you're so inclined you may leave out the liver and roe, although they are packed with clean lobster flavor.

Roast Corn Pudding

4 ears corn

6 cups / 1.5 L milk

4 tablespoons / 60 mL butter

1 large onion, minced

1 teaspoon / 5 mL cumin seeds

4 cloves garlic, minced

1 ½ cups / 375 mL cornmeal

1 teaspoon salt

Reserved lobster liver, roe, and knuckle meat

Make the corn cob broth by following the instructions in the smoked clam corn chowder recipe or by combining the corn cobs and milk for both recipes. Strain the corn broth and discard the cobs.

Meanwhile, in a large, heavy saucepan, melt the butter over medium heat. Add the onions and the corn kernels and, stirring constantly, cook them until caramelized.

Meanwhile, toast the cumin seed. Add the cumin seeds to a dry pan over high heat. Shake the pan until the seeds begin to brown slightly and give off a distinct aroma. This won't take long. Grind the cumin seed and add it with the garlic to the corn and onions. Sauté 1 minute.

Add the corn broth and bring it to a simmer. Add the salt. Add the cornmeal in a slow, steady stream, stirring it constantly with a whisk. As soon as all the cornmeal is added switch to a wooden spoon and add the reserved lobster parts.

Continue stirring until the mixture thickens and pulls away from the sides of the pot. Pour the mixture into an 8-inch/20 cm square shallow pan, pat it down evenly to a depth of 1 inch/2.5 cm, and place it in the refrigerator to firm up.

Once the pudding is firm, cut it into circles using a 3-inch/8 cm biscuit cutter.

Just before serving, reheat the puddings in a microwave or crisp in butter in a medium nonstick sauté pan until heated through.

This method is inspired by classic polenta. It takes advantage of the strong hidden corn flavors in the cob. Toasting the cumin seeds intensifies their aromatic flavors.

The Plate!

Ladle ½ cup/125 mL of the chowder into the center of each of 6 hot shallow soup plates. Add a small pile of tender pea shoots. Place a hot corn pudding on the shoots. Interlock pieces of the glazed lobster tail on top of the pudding. Place the claw meat in the chowder on opposite sides of the pudding. Top with some of the red pepper relish. Garnish with the reserved lobster antennas and a single pea shoot. Serve with a flourish!

Pea shoots

❖ LOBSTER ❖

Early European explorers to the New World were amazed to discover full-grown lobsters five to six feet long. Those sizes are impossible with today's efficient harvesting, and instead we consume relatively young specimens. Once they were so plentiful that they were fed to prisoners and spread on fields for fertilizer; now they command luxury prices. Somehow the lobster is able to transform its preferred diet of rotting fish into the sweet, firm flesh that connoisseurs enjoy.

Seaweed-Crusted Salmon
with Warm Tomato Vinaigrette and
Spinach Clam Risotto in an Asiago Crisp

Salmon's versatility is highlighted in this unique recipe, one of my favorite ways to cook the fish.
The amazing briny flavors of the seaweed steal the show and are guaranteed to make you a fan of this often
overlooked ingredient. The presentation is always a hit!

◇ 4 SERVINGS ◇

TIMING: MAKE THE ASIAGO CRISPS AND THE TOMATO VINAIGRETTE AHEAD. | MAKE THE RISOTTO.
| JUST BEFORE SERVING, COOK THE SALMON AND REHEAT THE VINAIGRETTE.

Asiago Crisps

1 cup / 250 mL grated asiago cheese

Note: This recipe relies on a nonstick silicone baking mat or a nonstick skillet.

Preheat the oven to 400°F/200°C. Line a large baking sheet with a nonstick baking mat.

Sprinkle the cheese in even 5-inch/12 cm circles on the baking mat, 1 inch/2.5 cm apart. Bake for several minutes, then peek at the cheese and continue cooking until the crisps are a uniform deep golden brown. Remove them from the oven as they brown with a small metal spatula and drape over a small inverted bowl to form a cup shape. When they are cool, remove them gently and store them in an airtight container.

Depending on your oven, some crisps may brown before others, so remove each one as it's done. Let the disks cool briefly before handling them so they don't tear. If they cool too much and won't mold, just reheat them briefly until they are pliable again.

Warm Tomato Vinaigrette

Purée all the ingredients until very smooth in a blender. Strain through a fine-mesh strainer. Store refrigerated.

Before serving, heat the sauce. Taste, and adjust seasonings.

The vinaigrette is heated at the last second to highlight the flavors of the tomatoes, so make sure they are perfect vine-ripened specimens.

2 very ripe tomatoes

½ cup / 125 mL extra virgin olive oil

½ cup / 125 mL red wine vinegar

1 teaspoon / 5 mL Tabasco® pepper sauce

Salt to taste

Seaweed-Crusted Salmon

Heat a thin layer of the olive oil in a nonstick sauté pan. Dredge the salmon fillets in the sea parsley and place in the pan. Cook, searing the parsley onto the fish, for several minutes until a peek reveals that the bottom is evenly cooked. Turn the fish and continue cooking until the salmon is just cooked through, 7 to 10 minutes in total. Serve immediately.

4 (6-ounce / 175 g) salmon fillets, skin removed

½ cup / 125 mL dried sea parsley powder*

Extra virgin olive oil for searing

*SEA PARSLEY POWDER IS AVAILABLE ONLY FROM OCEAN PRODUCE INTERNATIONAL IN NOVA SCOTIA. CALL 1-800-565-8773 TO ORDER.

Spinach Clam Risotto

FOR THE SPINACH PURÉE:

2 tablespoons / 25 mL extra virgin olive oil

1 shallot, minced

2 cloves garlic, minced

1 (10 ounce / 284 g) package spinach, cleaned

2 tablespoons / 25 mL water

FOR THE CLAM BROTH:

5 pounds / 2.2 kg littleneck or other steamer-type clams

¼ cup / 60 mL Chardonnay

FOR THE RISOTTO:

4 tablespoons / 60 mL butter

2 cups / 500 mL super-fino grade arborio rice

4 large shallots, minced

4 large cloves garlic, minced

1 cup / 250 mL Chardonnay

8 cups / 2 L reserved clam broth

1 cup / 250 mL flat-leaf parsley

1 cup / 250 mL grated awesome Parmesan cheese

Salt and pepper to taste

Make the spinach purée: In a large skillet, sauté the shallot and garlic in the olive oil until softened and fragrant. Add the spinach and water and stir just until the spinach wilts. Purée the spinach until very smooth in a food processor or in a blender. Reserve.

Make the clam broth: Place the clams and Chardonnay in a medium saucepan with a tight-fitting lid. Place the pan over high heat. The wine will steam and the clams will open, releasing their juices and heating through. After about 5 minutes, check on their progress and stop cooking them if they have all opened wide. Discard any clams that haven't opened. Shuck the clams and reserve the meat. Strain the cooking liquid and add enough water to it to equal 8 cups/2 L. Wipe out the saucepan and pour the clam broth into it. When you begin making the risotto, bring the broth to a simmer.

Make the risotto: Melt the butter in a medium, heavy saucepan over medium-high heat. Add the rice and the shallots and sauté, stirring, until the rice grains feel chalky and have a tiny white dot in their center. Don't brown the shallots. Add the garlic and sauté for 30 seconds.

Add the Chardonnay and reduce it by three-quarters, stirring constantly. Add enough of the clam broth to cover the rice and reduce the heat to just sustain a simmer. Continue stirring until all the broth is absorbed. Add more clam broth, just covering the rice, and simmer, stirring frequently. (Meanwhile, cook the salmon.)

Continue cooking the risotto and adding the broth until the rice is just done. It should be al dente: slightly firm, with each grain distinct and done to a pleasing texture but not mushy.

Stir in the reserved spinach purée, clams, parsley, and Parmesan. Season the risotto with salt and pepper. Stir just long enough to completely heat through. Serve immediately.

The method for proper risotto making coaxes out the high level of starch in the arborio grain, allowing it to thicken the surrounding cooking liquid to a creaminess unlike any other rice. Keeping the simmering temperature constant by adding already hot liquid helps the process. It is possible to cook the rice ahead of time two-thirds of the way, then finish it when ready.

The Plate!

Pour ¼ cup/60 mL of the just heated sauce into the center of 4 heated wide, shallow plates. Place an asiago crisp in the center of each plate. Spoon a heaping amount of the just-finished risotto into the crisp. Position a salmon fillet on the risotto. Serve with a splash!

◇ ARBORIO RICE ◇

Risotto and the arborio rice used to make it are two of the most defining contributions of Italy to global cuisine. The best grain for risotto is the "super-fino" grade medium-grain arborio. Its high level of starch is coaxed out during the slow cooking and thickens the surrounding liquid to a pleasant and characteristic creaminess. When cooked to perfection the grain is tender while retaining a distinct bite.

Pan-Seared Skate Wing
with Single Malt Scotch Lentils, Grilled Asparagus, Lentil Sprouts, and Brown Butter Sauce

Skate is one of the most distinctive fish I know. It's cheap, plentiful, and very tasty.
The captivating flavors in this presentation elevate it to a memorable status as a prime-time player!

◇ 4 SERVINGS ◇

TIMING: THE LENTIL SPROUTS MUST BE STARTED 5 TO 7 DAYS IN ADVANCE. | START THE LENTILS ABOUT AN HOUR AND A HALF AHEAD.
| AT THE LAST MINUTE GRILL THE ASPARAGUS AND COOK THE FISH AND THE SAUCE.

Lentil Sprouts

¼ cup / 60 mL dried lentils

Rinse the lentils thoroughly, removing any stones.

Place the lentils in a large canning jar with a tight-fitting two-piece lid. Cover them with several inches of room-temperature water, close the lid, and let rest at room temperature in a dark place.

The next day drain the water, rinse the lentils, refresh them in cool water, and drain them again. Let them rest in their dark hideaway. Rinse them twice a day, draining the water completely. As they begin to sprout, stop rinsing and just mist them with a sprayer so as not to disturb the fragile shoots.

After 5 days or so, when they have fully sprouted, place the jar in a sunny window for the day. The sprouts will begin to turn green and darken the longer they rest in the sun.

Don't overwater the sprouts. They only need to be damp to encourage their growth. You may have to pick out a few stray rotten seeds as they progress. The sprouts will be sweet and delicious when done.

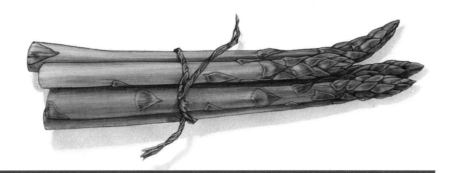

Scotch Lentils

Melt the butter in a medium saucepan. Add the onions and sauté them until they are golden brown, releasing and evaporating their liquid along the way.

Add the garlic and sauté a few minutes more. Add the lentils, the bay leaf, and the broth. Bring the mixture to a simmer and continue cooking, covered, over low heat. Cook until the lentils are tender but hold their shape, 20 to 30 minutes. Discard the bay leaf. Season with salt and pepper, and set aside.

Shortly before serving, gently reheat the lentils if needed. Stir in the scotch and serve immediately.

Don't overcook them; make sure they retain a pleasing "bite" but not a crunch. If they are soupy when done, turn up the heat, remove the cover, and quickly reduce the liquid.

1 tablespoon / 15 mL butter

1 cup / 250 mL minced onion

2 cloves garlic, minced

1 cup / 250 mL French green lentils

1 bay leaf

3 cups / 750 mL fish or chicken broth

Salt and pepper to taste

¼ cup / 60 mL single malt scotch

Skate and Brown Butter Sauce

Purée the lemon and capers in a food processor. Reserve the paste.

Make a series of ½-inch cuts along the edges of the skate fillet to help keep it from curling as it cooks. Melt the butter in a large, heavy nonstick skillet over medium-high heat. Meanwhile, dredge the fillets in the flour. Watch as the butter melts and begins to froth. When it begins to brown add the fillets and sear them on one side for 3 or 4 minutes until they are golden brown. Season on both sides as the fish cooks. (Meanwhile, begin the asparagus.) Flip them and sear on the second side just to cook the fish through. Skate cooks quickly because it is thin, so be vigilant!

Remove the fish to a platter and keep warm. Add the cream to the pan, turn up the heat, and boil until reduced by half. Stir in the reserved paste and chives, and serve immediately.

Zest and juice of 1 lemon

2 tablespoons / 25 mL capers

4 (6-ounce / 175 g) skate wing fillets, trimmed, with skin and sinew removed

¼ pound / 125 g butter (½ cup / 125 mL)

All-purpose flour for dredging

Salt and pepper to taste

1 cup / 250 mL heavy cream

¼ cup / 60 mL snipped chives

Asparagus

24 spears asparagus, ½ inch / 1 cm thick

4 tablespoons / 60 mL extra virgin olive oil

2 tablespoons / 25 mL Dijon mustard

Zest and juice of 2 lemons

Salt and pepper to taste

Trim off the woody bottom of the asparagus stems. Trim the spears so they are 5 inches/12 cm long.

Whisk together the oil, mustard, lemon zest, lemon juice, and salt and pepper until smooth.

In a steamer or microwave, cook the asparagus until it is half-cooked and has begun to deepen in color. Toss them in the lemon mixture. Place them on a grill and continue cooking them until just done, turning them over as needed and leaving characteristic grill marks on them.

The Plate!

While the fish cooks construct a stockade of the asparagus spears in the center of each of 4 hot large plates. Fill the asparagus crib with the just-finished lentils. Drape a wing of the skate over the lentils. Finish the sauce and artfully pour it over the fish. Add a flourish of sprouts to the top. Serve with a whoosh!

> ### ◈ LENTILS ◈
>
> *Man has enjoyed lentils for more than 8,000 years since first cultivating them in the Middle East. They are extremely nutritious and actually have more protein than beef. I enjoy them most because of their pleasant earthy flavor; they add a hearty note to whatever they grace. The best variety is the tiny dark green French lentil. Red lentils are also tasty, but they are lacking skin, so they cook to a mush and lose much of their color along the way.*

Campfire-style Rainbow Trout
with Roast Potato Salad, Homemade Ketchup,
and Pickled Rhubarb

When I was a kid my dad would take us fishing, and this dish reminds me of the flavors at the end of the day. It's a sophisticated picnic on a plate, only now forks and napkins are required. Ah, progress!

◈ 4 SERVINGS, WITH LEFTOVER KETCHUP ◈

TIMING: MAKE THE KETCHUP THE DAY BEFORE. | START THE POTATO SALAD SEVERAL HOURS BEFORE.
| COOK THE FISH AND PICKLE THE RHUBARB AT THE LAST MINUTE.

Ketchup

Purée the tomatoes, onions, vinegar, and oil in a blender, in batches if necessary. Pour the purée into a large, heavy saucepan.

Add the remaining ingredients and bring the mixture to a boil. Reduce the heat and let the mixture simmer, stirring frequently, until it has reduced by three-quarters. This may take an hour or more.

Remove the bay leaves and purée the ketchup again in a blender until very smooth.

Pour into a squeeze bottle and reserve for garnishing the plates. Any extra ketchup will keep for several weeks in your refrigerator.

This ketchup must reduce quite a bit to thicken, but don't let it stick and burn as it does. Its flavors will mellow and combine as it rests for several days.

4 pounds / 2 kg ripe tomatoes

1 pound / 500 g onions, chopped

2 cups / 500 mL cider vinegar

½ cup / 125 mL extra virgin olive oil

1 cup / 250 mL sugar

½ cup / 125 mL tomato paste

1 teaspoon / 5 mL salt

½ teaspoon / 2 mL dry mustard

½ teaspoon / 2 mL paprika

½ teaspoon / 2 mL ground allspice

½ teaspoon / 2 mL ground cloves

½ teaspoon / 2 mL cinnamon

½ teaspoon / 2 mL freshly grated nutmeg

2 bay leaves

Roast Potato Salad

8 slices bacon, chopped

½ cup / 125 mL water

1 pound / 500 g new potatoes, halved

1 large onion, sliced

4 tablespoons / 60 mL red wine vinegar

1 tablespoon / 15 mL whole grain mustard

1 teaspoon / 5 mL sugar

2 tablespoons / 25 mL finely chopped parsley

Salt and pepper

Preheat the oven to 400°F/200°C. Place the bacon and water in a skillet and bring to a simmer. Continue simmering until the water evaporates and the bacon begins to crisp. When it is fully crisp, strain the fat into a roasting pan. Reserve the crisp bacon.

Add the potatoes and onion slices to the bacon fat in the roasting pan. Toss them, coating them well with the fat. Roast the potatoes until they are golden brown, about 30 minutes, stirring every few minutes so the potatoes cook evenly.

Combine the vinegar, mustard, and sugar. Toss the potatoes with the vinegar dressing, the bacon, and the parsley. Season them to taste with salt and pepper. If you prefer, the salad may cool to room temperature before you serve it.

The key to the depth of flavor in this salad is the roasting of the potato. Use a pan big enough that they make a single layer and roast evenly. Be vigilant and patient.

Pickled Rhubarb

2 cups / 500 mL white wine vinegar

1 cup / 250 mL sugar

1 tablespoon / 15 mL ground star anise

1 large stalk rhubarb, cut into 4-inch / 10 cm pieces then halved lengthwise

Combine the vinegar, sugar, and star anise in a medium saucepan. Bring the mixture to a simmer, stirring so the sugar dissolves.

A few minutes before serving, add the rhubarb pieces to the syrup and let them simmer until soft, 1 to 2 minutes. Serve immediately.

To improve the star anise flavor, let the syrup rest for 60 minutes or so before adding the rhubarb.

Campfire-style Rainbow Trout

Fillet the trout by first removing the head then the two fillets. Trim off the belly bones of each fillet. Do not remove the skin. Alternatively, purchase 4 skin-on fillets.

Season the cornmeal with salt and pepper. Lightly press the skin side of the fillets into the cornmeal.

Soak a large handful of hardwood chips in water for a few minutes. Smoke the trout fillets: Using 2 metal pans of equal size, make a stovetop smoker. Fill the bottom of one pan with wood chips. Place a lightly oiled cooling rack over the pan. Invert the second pan over the rack, creating a smoking chamber. Place the smoker over medium heat until the wood chips begin to smoke. Place the trout fillets on the screen and smoke for 60 seconds. Make sure you have good ventilation or do this outdoors; it will generate a lot of smoke.

Melt the butter in a cast-iron skillet or sauté pan over medium heat. When it begins to foam add the trout fillets, skin side down, and fry them for 3 to 4 minutes. Flip the fillets and fry 1 to 2 minutes on the other side. (Meanwhile, poach the rhubarb.) Serve immediately.

You may skip the smoking step. The skin side takes longer to cook than the other. After you flip the fish it is done almost immediately, so be ready to plate!

2 rainbow trout (about 3 pounds / 1.5 kg each), dressed and cleaned (or 4 skin-on fillets)

1 cup / 250 mL cornmeal

Salt and pepper to taste

2 tablespoons / 25 mL butter

The Plate!

Parsley sprigs

Squeeze some of the ketchup decoratively onto each of 4 hot dinner plates. Add a pile of the potato salad. Cut each trout fillet in half. Arrange one half skin side down on the plate and top with the second half skin side up. Add some just poached rhubarb and garnish with a parsley sprig. Serve with a flourish!

> ### ◇ RHUBARB ◇
>
> *One of the first plants to pop up in the garden every year, rhubarb is often known as the pie plant because of its affinity for sugar and its most common use. Today's trendy chefs serve it with fish, not realizing that Auguste Escoffier himself advocated this pairing in his 1907 classic* Le Guide Culinaire. *Its pleasing tartness and affinity for exotic spices make it a favorite in my kitchen. Don't eat the leaves: they are laden with poisonous oxalic acid.*

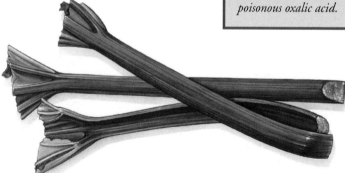

Smoked Salmon and Dill Roulade with Whole-Wheat Pancakes, Salmon Caviar, and Dandelion Greens Salad
(page 68)

Cinnamon Sweetbread and Pine Nut Crisp Stack
with Warm Carrot Olive Oil Emulsion, Basil Coulis,
and Balsamic Vinegar Glazed Carrots
(page 74)

Seaweed-Crusted Salmon with
Warm Tomato Vinaigrette and
Spinach Clam Risotto in an Asiago Crisp
(page 86)

Potato-Crusted Monkfish with Chive Oyster Gravy and a Melted Onion Leek Tart *(page 100)*

Just Baked Salmon
with Roast Carrot Sauce, Salmon Seviche, Juniper Pickled Red Onions, and Watercress Salad

A cook who can leave the center of a salmon fillet opaque, pink, and just barely heated deserves respect. This method treats the whole fillet that way, a real treat for fans of salmon's richness. The other flavors on the plate are crisp and bright, making this one of my favorites!

◇ 4 SERVINGS ◇

TIMING: MAKE THE PICKLED ONION AND REFRIGERATE AT LEAST 12 HOURS. | MAKE THE SEVICHE AND REFRIGERATE SEVERAL HOURS. | MAKE THE CARROT SAUCE. | MAKE THE SALAD. | WHILE YOU ARE BAKING THE SALMON, REHEAT THE SAUCE AND TOSS THE SALAD.

Juniper Pickled Red Onions

Use a small electric coffee grinder to grind the juniper berries, or place them in a clean towel and crush them with a hammer. Combine the berries with the sugar and vinegar in a small saucepan. Bring the berry mixture to a simmer, stirring to dissolve the sugar, and cook it gently for 5 minutes. Turn off the heat, add the Tabasco®, and let the syrup stand for 30 minutes. Strain it to remove any juniper pieces and bring it to a simmer once more.

Place the onion rings in a nonreactive container and pour the syrup over them. Cover the onion mixture and refrigerate it overnight. Shake frequently.

3 tablespoons / 45 mL whole juniper berries

1 cup / 250 mL sugar

1 cup / 250 mL red wine vinegar

1 teaspoon / 5 mL Tabasco® pepper sauce

1 large red onion, sliced into thin rings

Salmon Seviche

Roughly chop the salmon scraps. Combine them with the remaining ingredients and toss them until they are well combined.

Let the seviche rest, refrigerated, for several hours for the flavors to blend together.

The lime juice is so acidic that it actually cooks the salmon, affecting its proteins in much the same way heat does. Trim the salmon of any skin or darker meat beforehand.

4 to 6 ounces / 125 to 175 g salmon scraps reserved from the fillets

½ cup / 125 mL fresh lime juice

Zest from the juiced limes

2 tablespoons / 25 mL extra virgin olive oil

¼ cup / 60 mL snipped chives

Salt and pepper to taste

Roast Carrot Sauce

4 tablespoons / 60 mL extra virgin olive oil

2 cups / 500 mL diced carrot

3 cups / 750 mL carrot juice

½ teaspoon / 2 mL salt

In a nonstick sauté pan, heat the oil over medium heat. Add the carrots and sauté until golden brown and caramelized. Add 1 cup of the carrot juice, cover the pan, and simmer for 10 minutes until the carrots soften. Uncover and reduce the juice until completely evaporated.

Place the roasted carrots in a blender with the remaining carrot juice and salt, and purée until very smooth. Strain the sauce through a fine-mesh strainer. Reserve.

Warm the sauce before serving.

Watercress Salad

¼ cup / 60 mL finely diced carrot

4 tablespoons / 60 mL extra virgin olive oil

4 tablespoons / 60 mL lime juice

Several handfuls of watercress, tough stems removed

In a small saucepan, heat the carrots with the olive oil. Stir in the lime juice. Reserve.

When ready to serve, toss with the watercress.

Just Baked Salmon

4 (6-ounce / 175 g) salmon fillets, evenly thick (1½ to 2 inches / 4 to 5 cm), skin removed

2 tablespoons / 25 mL extra virgin olive oil

½ teaspoon / 2 mL Bay Fortune seasoning (page 40)

Coarse sea salt

Preheat the oven to 250°F/120°C. If needed, trim the fillets so they are evenly thick.

Mix together the oil and seasoning. Rub each of the salmon fillets with the oil mixture until evenly coated. Place the fillets on a baking pan in the center of the oven, and bake for 15 to 20 minutes until each fillet is heated through and just cooked. (Warm the carrot sauce and toss the salad as the salmon bakes.) Sprinkle with coarse sea salt and serve immediately.

If the salmon fillet has a thinner end, trim it off and use it in the seviche or tuck it under the thicker part before baking. The salmon will have a faintly translucent look to it when it's done, and will flake easily. If there are any white spots on its surface, it has been overcooked: they are interior juices coagulating on the surface. The slow baking time is meant only to heat the salmon through and will give it a melt-in-the-mouth texture. Ovens vary, so check the fish after 15 minutes — it may be done. After 20 minutes, it's done.

The Plate!

Ladle ¼ cup/60 mL of the carrot sauce onto each of 4 warm plates. Mold the seviche in a ring mold 3 inches/8 cm wide by 1 inch/2.5 cm tall, and transfer to the plate with a small spatula. Remove the mold.

Watercress sprigs

Place a pile of the salad on the seviche. Gently position a salmon fillet on the salad. Top with some pickled red onions and a watercress sprig. Serve with a flourish!

◇ WATERCRESS ◇

The best watercress grows wild in freshwater streams and along their banks in late spring and early summer. It is a close relative of the nasturtium commonly found in flower gardens. Watercress's flavor is pleasingly peppery with a mildly bitter aftertaste, making it an excellent foil for rich ingredients. It has a cooling effect in the mouth rather than the heating effect its flavors would suggest.

Potato-Crusted Monkfish
with Chive Oyster Gravy and a
Melted Onion Leek Tart

I love simple cooking methods that leave guests wondering "How'd you do that?" Although this recipe depends on a specific tool, the results are worth the expense. It's also a chance to show off the glorious results of patience combined with slow-cooking onions.

◇ 4 SERVINGS ◇

TIMING: MAKE THE CHIVE ESSENCE FOR GARNISH SEVERAL DAYS AHEAD. | START THE ONIONS FOR THE TARTS SEVERAL HOURS IN ADVANCE. | START THE GRAVY SEVERAL HOURS IN ADVANCE. | AS THE TARTS ARE FINISHING, FINISH THE GRAVY AND COOK THE FISH.

Melted Onion Leek Tarts

¼ pound / 125 g butter (½ cup / 125 mL)

5 pounds / 2.2 kg onions, thinly sliced

2 leeks, white stalks thinly sliced, green leaves left whole

1 teaspoon / 5 mL freshly ground nutmeg

1 cup / 250 mL heavy cream

Salt and pepper to taste

2 eggs

Melt the butter in a large, heavy sauté pan over high heat. Add the onions and sliced leek stalks. Cook the vegetables, stirring frequently, as they release their moisture and the water steams them. Gradually the liquid will evaporate and the vegetables will begin to change color. Turn the heat down gradually to medium-low and stir frequently as the onions slowly become a rich golden brown. This will take at least an hour and as many as several hours to do properly. Take your time and do not burn the vegetables. Try to preserve the shape of the vegetables as much as possible. The vegetables will reduce in volume 10 times!

Stir in the nutmeg for a few minutes. Stir in the cream and reduce it by half. Remove the pan from the heat and let the mixture cool for a few minutes. (The onion mixture may be prepared ahead to this point.) Taste and season.

Preheat the oven to 350°F/180°C. Line a baking sheet with parchment paper.

Season the leek leaves with salt and pepper, then steam or microwave them until they soften and turn brighter green. Butter 4 ring molds 3 inches/8 cm wide by 1½ inches/4 cm tall. Set them in the baking pan. Fit the leek leaves snugly and evenly into the molds, overlapping on the bottom and slightly around the edges. Trim the ends so they fold back perfectly.

Whisk the eggs and gently stir them into the cooled onion mixture. Divide the mixture evenly among the molds, just filling them. Fold the overhanging ends back to snugly cover the top. Dot with butter and fit a 3-inch/8 cm disk of parchment paper on them. Bake the tarts for 15 minutes or until the custard is set.

Let the tarts rest briefly or serve immediately.

Be patient — the onions may need several hours to cook properly. The moist heat-steaming of the tarts preserves the bright green of the leek leaves. Leeks can be very sandy; rinse them very well in several changes of water.

Chive Oyster Gravy

Melt the butter in a large, heavy saucepan, add the onions, and cook them as for the melted onions in the preceding recipe. When they are golden brown, add the garlic and cook for a few more minutes. Stir in the wine and reduce it by three-quarters. Stir in the cream and reduce it by half. Purée the mixture in a blender. Set aside.

While the fish is cooking, gently reheat the gravy. Add the chives, the oysters, and their liquor and just heat through. Season with salt and pepper. Serve immediately.

This method is designed not to overcook the oysters. The meat should just be heated through and not allowed to simmer or it will shrink and toughen.

4 tablespoons / 60 mL butter

2 large onions, sliced

1 head garlic, peeled and minced (less if you prefer)

1 cup / 250 mL Chardonnay

2 cups / 500 mL heavy cream

½ cup / 125 mL minced chives

16 oysters, freshly shucked, liquor strained and reserved

Salt and pepper to taste

Potato-Crusted Monkfish

2 large peeled potatoes

4 (6-ounce / 175 g) monkfish fillets,
cleaned and trimmed

¼ cup / 60 mL clarified butter

Salt and pepper to taste

Note: This recipe uses a Japanese Benriner potato turning device.

Load the potatoes onto the Benriner and cut into long thin curly strands. Carefully wrap them evenly and completely around the fish. Secure the ends of the strands under themselves.

Brown the potato-wrapped fish evenly in the clarified butter in a medium nonstick skillet over medium-high heat until the potato is crisp and evenly golden brown. Probe the fish for doneness and bake briefly in a preheated 400°F/200°C oven if needed. Season and serve immediately.

If you don't have a potato turner, try using a channel knife on a peeled potato — or skip the potato crust.

The Plate!

Chive essence (page 38)

Chives

Place a just-baked onion leek tart in the center of each of 4 heated large, shallow soup or pasta bowls. Ladle ¼ cup/60 mL of the oyster gravy over the tart. Position a potato-wrapped fillet on it. Add several chives and some chive oil puddles. Serve with a fish face!

◈ LEEKS ◈

The leek, which looks like a giant green onion, is much milder and subtler in flavor than its cousin the onion. Its white base results from the practice of piling soil around it as it grows, preventing the sun from forming green chlorophyll. This also explains its tendency to be very sandy inside. They are one of the pillars of classic French cuisine, where they are sometimes referred to as poor man's asparagus.

Saffron-Poached Halibut
with Tomato Sambuca Sauce, Roast Fennel,
and Dried Tomato Tapenade

As a chef I am inspired by the authenticity of cooks everywhere. This presentation is derived from the classic flavors of bouillabaisse. Tradition and careful cooking methods combine to form a new classic.

◇ 4 SERVINGS ◇

TIMING: MAKE THE TAPENADE UP TO A DAY AHEAD. | MAKE THE TOMATO SAUCE A DAY AHEAD. | ROAST THE FENNEL AN HOUR OR SO AHEAD.
| REHEAT THE SAUCE AND THE FENNEL WHILE POACHING THE FISH.

Dried Tomato Tapenade

Place all the ingredients in a food processor and process until very well combined but still slightly coarse. Reserve until needed.

Regular canned black olives are too bland for this recipe, whereas kalamata-style olives are strongly flavored and define this condiment.

2 cups / 500 mL pitted cured black olives

4 anchovy fillets

1 cup / 250 mL dried tomatoes
(softened in water if stiff)

4 tablespoons / 60 mL extra virgin olive oil

Zest and juice of 1 lemon

2 garlic cloves, minced

1 cup / 250 mL parsley

Salt and pepper to taste

Saffron-Poached Halibut

Combine the broth, wine, lemon juice, lemon zest, and saffron in a pot just large enough to hold the fish in a single layer. Bring the mixture to a simmer and simmer for 10 minutes. Taste and season with salt.

Gently place the fish in the simmering liquid. Cook just until done, 8 to 10 minutes.

continued >>

3 cups / 750 mL white fish broth or water

1 cup / 250 mL Chardonnay

Zest and juice of 1 lemon

1 teaspoon / 5 mL saffron threads

Salt

4 (6-ounce / 175 g) halibut fillets

Remove from the broth and serve immediately. (The broth may be reserved for another use. Bring it to a full boil, then cool and refrigerate or freeze it.)

Simmering the poaching liquid first allows the saffron to fully develop its flavors before being introduced to the halibut. The fish should be fully submerged to poach properly. Don't boil the broth as the fish cooks — this is a gentle method.

Tomato Sambuca Sauce

1 tablespoon / 15 mL extra virgin olive oil

1 cup / 250 mL minced onion

1 cup / 250 mL minced fennel

2 cloves garlic, minced

½ cup / 125 mL Sambuca

2 large very ripe tomatoes, chopped

1 cup / 250 mL white fish broth

1 teaspoon / 5 mL cayenne Tabasco® pepper sauce

Salt

In a large skillet, sauté the onion and fennel in the olive oil until lightly browned. Add the garlic and cook a few minutes longer. Add the Sambuca, tomatoes, fish broth, and Tabasco®. Bring the mixture to a gentle simmer. Continue simmering gently for about 20 minutes as the vegetables soften.

Purée the sauce in a blender until smooth and set aside.

Shortly before serving, reheat the sauce and season with salt and more Tabasco® if needed. If necessary, thin it with some of the fish poaching liquid.

If you don't have fish broth try chicken broth. Try not to reduce the sauce as it simmers; that step is just for softening the vegetables.

Roast Fennel

Preheat the oven to 400°F/200°C.

Trim the stalks from the fennel bulb and reserve for another use. Reserve some of the fronds for the garnish. Cut the bulb in half and cut out the tough woody center. Cut the fennel into ½-inch/1 cm thick slices and lay in a single layer on a baking sheet that has been brushed liberally with olive oil. Brush the top of the fennel slices with oil and season thoroughly with the fennel seed and salt and pepper.

Roast for 15 to 20 minutes until the slices begin to brown. Flip them and continue roasting for another 15 to 20 minutes. Set aside until needed. At the last second reheat in a microwave and toss with the cilantro.

1 fennel bulb

4 tablespoons / 60 mL extra virgin olive oil

1 tablespoon / 15 mL ground fennel seed

Salt and pepper to taste

¼ cup / 60 mL chopped cilantro

The Plate!

Ladle ¼ cup/60 mL of the hot tomato sauce onto each of 4 heated plates. Place a neat pile of the roasted fennel in the center of the plate. Place a poached halibut fillet on top of the fennel. Top with a spoonful of the tapenade. Garnish with some reserved fennel fronds. Serve with a splash!

◈ TOMATOES ◈

Because of its membership in the deadly nightshade family, tomato, upon its discovery in the New World, was thought to be poisonous. The Italians quickly realized otherwise, and now this fruit is an integral part of their cuisine. Unfortunately, today the vast majority of the crop is picked hard and green and shipped great distances before being artificially ripened. The result is a hard, flavorless object touted as a tomato. If you don't have access to the sun-ripened warm-from-the-vine real thing, then canned tomatoes, which are left on the vine to ripen before processing, are your best option.

Prosciutto Roast Cod with Preserved Lemon Squeeze, Roasted Tomato Rosemary Sauce, Wilted Spinach, and Israeli Couscous with Parmesan

I am a huge fan of global cuisine, traveling and tasting every chance I get.
Morocco has one of the most diverse and fascinating culinary heritages of any culture.
You won't find this dish there, but you will find the inspiration for its exotic flavors.

◇ 4 SERVINGS, WITH LEFTOVER PRESERVED LEMONS ◇

TIMING: MAKE THE LEMONS AT LEAST A MONTH IN ADVANCE. | MAKE THE TOMATO SAUCE ABOUT AN HOUR AHEAD.
| WHILE THE COUSCOUS SITS, REHEAT THE SAUCE, WILT THE SPINACH, AND WRAP AND ROAST THE FISH.

Preserved Lemons

⅓ cup / 75 mL salt

2 pounds / 1 kg fresh, ripe, juicy lemons

Extra lemons for juice

FOR THE COMPOTE:

½ teaspoon / 2 mL Tabasco® pepper sauce

4 tablespoons / 60 mL extra virgin olive oil

Sterilize a wide-mouthed jar with a tight-fitting lid. Spoon 2 tablespoons/ 25 mL of salt into the jar and shake it around.

Wash the lemons in warm water and rinse them well. Remove the stem remnants. Place the lemons in a 400°F/200°C oven for several minutes, warming and drying the skin.

Roll each lemon vigorously on the counter for a moment to soften it up. Cut each lemon lengthwise into quarters, stopping ½ inch/ 1 cm or so before the stem end. Open up the lemons and sprinkle the insides with salt, then squeeze them tightly over a sieve set over a bowl to release as much of their juice as possible. Reserve the juice and discard all seeds. Place the lemons in the jar, sprinkling some salt on each layer and using the salt up by the top layer. Add the lemon juice as you go and shake the jar a bit to dislodge any air bubbles. Fill the jar as close to the top as possible.

Fold a square of plastic wrap in four. Fit it over the rim of the jar and close the lid tightly. Place the jar in a warm, sunny place and let it rest for a month or so. Every day shake it a bit to redistribute the curing and preserving brine. Refrigerate after opening the jar for the first time.

To make the compote squeeze for this dish, take 2 of the lemons and place in a food processor or blender with the Tabasco® and olive oil. Process until smooth and reserve in a squeeze bottle.

Pick out any seeds in the lemons. Experiment with adding your favorite aromatics, such as bay leaves or cloves, to the lemons as they cure. Their best flavor is realized after one month, when they become very fragrant and lose the characteristic bitterness of the skin.

Roasted Tomato Rosemary Sauce

Preheat the oven to 400°F/200°C.

In a roasting pan, toss together the tomatoes, onion, garlic, oil, and rosemary. Spread them into a single layer and season with salt and pepper. Roast for 30 to 45 minutes, shaking the pan every few minutes until the vegetables are nicely caramelized but not burnt.

Place the vegetables in a blender. Add the broth to the roasting pan and stir over medium-high heat until all the remaining drippings are dissolved. Add this mixture to the blender and process until very smooth. Strain through a fine-mesh strainer and reserve in a small saucepan.

This recipe is meant to highlight the caramelized flavors of properly roasted tomatoes. Plum-type varieties work best as they have more flesh and less liquid than other kinds.

6 plum tomatoes, quartered

1 large onion, chopped

1 head garlic, peeled

½ cup / 125 mL extra virgin olive oil

1 tablespoon / 15 mL minced fresh rosemary

Salt and pepper to taste

1 cup / 250 mL fish or light chicken broth

Israeli Couscous

2 tablespoons / 25 mL extra virgin olive oil

½ cup / 125 mL minced onion

2 cloves garlic, minced

1 cup / 250 mL Israeli couscous

½ cup / 125 mL Chardonnay

2 cups / 500 mL fish or chicken broth

½ cup / 125 mL grated Parmesan cheese

Salt and pepper to taste

In a small saucepan, sauté the onion and garlic in the olive oil until the onion is softened and translucent. Add the couscous and wine and stir briefly. Add the broth, cover the pot tightly, and reduce the heat to low, until the couscous absorbs the broth and cooks through, about 20 to 30 minutes.

Add the cheese and stir to combine. Season with salt and pepper and serve immediately.

Israeli couscous grains are much larger than regular grains and require more cooking. If you use regular couscous, bring the mixture to a boil, turn off the heat, and let rest 10 minutes before continuing.

Prosciutto Roast Cod

4 (6-ounce / 175 g) cod fillets

Salt and pepper to taste

8 ounces / 250 g thinly sliced prosciutto

4 tablespoons / 60 mL olive oil

Season the fillets with salt and pepper and tightly wrap them with the prosciutto. Wrap twice so as to cover the whole fish. Fasten with toothpicks if necessary.

Heat the oil in a large, heavy skillet until it just begins to smoke. Add the fish and brown it on all sides. Depending on its thickness, the fish will require 10 to 15 minutes of cooking in total. (Meanwhile, reheat the sauce and wilt the spinach.) If the prosciutto has browned but the fish is not cooked through, finish cooking the fish in a preheated 400°F/200°C oven. Serve immediately.

Wilted Spinach

Place the oil, prosciutto, and garlic in a sauté pan. Heat the oil gently, toasting the garlic and prosciutto. Add the spinach and broth and continue stirring as it wilts. Season with salt and pepper and serve immediately.

2 tablespoons / 25 mL extra virgin olive oil

3 ounces / 75 g prosciutto, cut into very thin strips

1 tablespoon / 15 mL minced garlic

6 ounces / 175 g spinach leaves, cleaned stems removed (2 cups / 500 mL)

2 tablespoons / 25 mL fish broth or white wine

Salt and pepper to taste

The Plate!

Form a ring of couscous in the center of each of 4 heated plates using a 3-inch/ 8 cm biscuit cutter or ring mold. Top with some wilted spinach. Center a piece of the fish on the spinach. Ladle some of the sauce over the fish. Garnish with the lemon squeeze and a sprig of rosemary. Serve with a flourish!

Rosemary sprigs

◈ ROSEMARY ◈

Rosemary is a perennial shrub and a member of the evergreen family. Its intense fragrance is incense-like in character and adds a delightful woodiness to any dish it accompanies. It has a long and colorful history as an important medicinal herb and supposedly warded off evil kitchen spirits. It is also a symbol of remembrance, friendship, and love, which explains why brides commonly carried it.

Smoked Salmon Ravioli
with Lemon Dijon Cream, Red Onions, Dill, and Salmon Caviar

I love the simplicity of pasta and the way it combines so easily with many flavors.
The richness of smoked salmon defines this luxurious and easy-to-make dish. Its classic partners
make this group of flavors familiar yet distinctive.

◇ 4 SERVINGS ◇

Smoked Salmon Ravioli with Lemon Dijon Cream and Red Onions

8 ounces / 250 g smoked salmon pieces

4 ounces / 125 g cream cheese

Salt and pepper to taste

8 (4-inch / 10 cm) fresh pasta squares

Semolina flour or cornmeal for dusting

1 tablespoon / 15 mL butter

¼ cup / 60 mL minced red onion

Zest and juice of 2 lemons

2 tablespoons / 25 mL coarse grain mustard

1 tablespoon / 15 mL Dijon mustard

1 cup / 250 mL heavy cream

Purée the smoked salmon and cream cheese in a food processor until smooth. Season with salt and pepper. Place a large spoonful of the mixture on the center of each pasta square. Moisten your fingers and rub around the edges of the pasta until it is slightly sticky. Fold over the square to form a large triangle. With your fingers force out any air pockets and press the filling into an even layer, leaving a 1-inch/ 2.5 cm border. Pinch the edges tightly together to seal the raviolis. Let the raviolis dry for several hours to strengthen the seal: sprinkle them with semolina flour or cornmeal and rest on wax paper in an airtight container.

Heat a medium saucepan over medium-high heat. Add the butter and red onions and sauté them until the onions are softened. Stir in the lemon juice, the mustards, and cream. Continue simmering until the mixture is reduced by half. Season it with salt and pepper.

While the sauce reduces, bring a large pot of water to a gentle rolling boil. Season it heavily with salt; it should taste pleasantly salty. Add the raviolis and cook until the pasta is just done and the contents are heated through, about 5 minutes. Remove the raviolis with a strainer and drain them well.

Moistening the pasta makes it sticky and helps to bind it together. Taste the cooking water; it should taste properly seasoned. If so the pasta, which absorbs water as it cooks, will also taste properly seasoned.

The Plate!

Pour a quarter of the sauce into each of 4 heated shallow pasta bowls. Place two of the raviolis in the sauce with one overlapping the other. Top with a scoop of the salmon caviar and a small pile of dill fronds. Sprinkle with the lemon zest. Serve with a mmm!

2 ounces / 50 g salmon caviar
½ cup / 125 mL whole dill fronds
Reserved lemon zest

◈ DILL ◈

As an apprentice cook in a rather average restaurant I was impressed by the chef's use of spindly dill fronds on every plate instead of ubiquitous parsley. At the time I thought I was in gourmet heaven — how chic! Today I garnish a plate with a particular herb only if that herb plays a role in the preparation. I have also learned to prize dill for its subtle tanginess and its gorgeously flimsy sprigs. Ah, progress . . .

Blue Cheese–Crusted Beef Tenderloin with Cabernet Sauvignon Sauce, Horseradish Potatoes, and Crisp Onion Rings

Here's a way to satisfy your guests' primal craving for beef and your desire to innovate: meat and potatoes with a twist! It's best not to get between this dish and carnivores familiar with its typical flavor partners.

◇ 4 SERVINGS ◇

TIMING: MAKE THE SAUCE AND KEEP WARM. | MAKE THE POTATOES AND KEEP WARM. | BAKE THE STEAK. | FRY THE ONION RINGS.

Cabernet Sauvignon Sauce

2 cups / 500 mL Cabernet Sauvignon

2 cups / 500 mL heavy cream

1 cup / 250 mL minced shallots

2 cloves garlic, minced

½ teaspoon / 2 mL minced rosemary

½ teaspoon / 2 mL salt

¼ teaspoon / 1 mL pepper

Place the wine, cream, shallots, garlic, rosemary, salt, and pepper in a saucepan and bring to a boil. Reduce the heat and simmer the sauce for 20 to 30 minutes until it has reduced by half and the vegetables are tender.

Pour the sauce into a blender and purée for several minutes until it is very smooth. Strain the sauce through a fine-mesh strainer. Keep the sauce warm until needed.

The key to the sauce is the reduction of the wine and cream, which intensifies the flavor almost to the full flavor of the wine used. Virtually any wine will work with this method because the other ingredients do not overwhelm the flavor of the wine. The puréed, tender vegetables are the thickening agent for the sauce.

Horseradish Potatoes

2 cups / 500 mL heavy cream

½ cup / 125 mL freshly grated horseradish (you may substitute prepared)

½ nutmeg nut

Place the cream and the horseradish in a small saucepan. Grate the nutmeg over the cream. Simmer the mixture, stirring occasionally, for 20 minutes or until it reduces to 1 cup/250 mL.

Preheat the oven to 400°F/200°C.

Steam the potatoes until tender. Pass them through a food mill onto a baking sheet and dry them for several minutes in the oven.

1 pound / 500 g potatoes, peeled and quartered

Salt and pepper to taste

Quickly and thoroughly combine the potatoes and the cream mixture in the bowl of a standing mixer fitted with a paddle (or in a large bowl with a wooden spoon). Season with salt and pepper. Serve immediately or keep warm, tightly covered in foil, in the oven as the beef finishes baking. When the beef is done, turn off the oven.

Blue Cheese–Crusted Beef Tenderloin

Preheat the oven to 400°F/200°C.

In a food processor, process the blue cheese and the ¼ pound/125 g of butter into a smooth paste. Add the bread crumbs and rosemary, and continue processing until thoroughly combined. Set aside.

Evenly coat each of the steaks with pepper, pressing it into the meat. Melt the remaining butter in a 10-inch/25 cm nonstick skillet. When the butter begins to foam, place the steaks in the pan. Sear each side of the steaks, turning them once as they brown. Watch carefully as you sear the meat and brown the butter. If the butter seems to be getting too hot, either turn the heat down slightly or baste the meat with several spoonfuls of the hot butter. (Meanwhile, begin heating the oil for the onion rings.) When the steaks are evenly seared, place them on a cooling or roasting rack.

Pat an even layer of the blue cheese paste onto the top of each steak. The paste should cover the entire top and extend slightly over the edges. Place the rack on a baking pan in the oven, and bake 10 to 15 minutes until the crust browns. (Meanwhile, fry the onion rings.) Let the steaks stand for 5 to 10 minutes before cutting them.

¼ pound / 125 g crumbled blue cheese

¼ pound / 125 g plus 2 tablespoons / 25 g butter, at room temperature (½ cup / 125 mL plus 2 tablespoons / 25 mL)

½ cup / 125 mL coarse dried bread crumbs

1 teaspoon / 5 mL minced rosemary

4 beef tenderloin steaks (about 6 ounces / 175 g each), chilled

1 tablespoon / 15 mL pepper

Crisp Onion Rings

4 cups / 1 L vegetable oil

1 cup / 250 mL all-purpose flour

1 teaspoon / 5 mL salt

1 teaspoon / 5 mL pepper

1 onion, thinly sliced into rings

In a high-sided pan, heat the oil until it reaches 360°F/185 °C. Meanwhile, in a large bowl combine the flour, salt, and pepper. Add the onions and toss until evenly coated with the seasoned flour. Fry the rings in batches until crisp and golden.

Drain on paper towels and serve immediately.

Vegetable oil works well, but for extra-special flavor fry the onions in rendered beef fat.

The Plate!

Ladle ¼ cup/60 mL of the hot sauce onto each of 4 hot plates. Place a 3 to 4-inch/8 to 10 cm wide by 1 to 2-inch/2.5 to 5 cm tall ring mold on a small plate and stuff it with the potatoes. With a small spatula, transfer the ring mold to the center of the serving plate, then remove the mold. Add a tenderloin and top with a pile of the crisp onions. Serve with a moo!

◇ BLUE CHEESE ◇

The blue cheeses of the world rank as some of the most aggressively flavored ingredients in my kitchen. England's Stilton, France's Roquefort, Italy's Gorgonzola, and America's Maytag are some notable examples. All blue cheeses are exposed to a specific penicillin-type mold that is sometimes grown on bread first, then ground and sprinkled on the curds as they are formed into wheels. They also need air as they cure, hence the pierce marks of needles that allow the air to penetrate the curing cheese.

Tomato Parmesan–Crusted Rack of Lamb with Tomato Mint Sauce and a Cinnamon Eggplant "Caviar" Tart

Rack of lamb is one of the most elegant meat presentations I know. In honor of its extravagance I always serve it with flair. This Mediterranean-influenced presentation reassures with its classic mint flavors and highlights the silky smoothness of eggplant as it creates a memorable frame for the lamb.

◇ 4 SERVINGS ◇

TIMING: MAKE THE EGGPLANT TARTS AND THE SAUCE AHEAD. | REHEAT THE TARTS AND THE SAUCE WHILE THE ROASTED LAMB RESTS.

Cinnamon Eggplant "Caviar" Tart

Note: Eggplant "caviar" is a traditional poor man's caviar substitute from Russia, the home of real caviar. Mashed eggplant vaguely resembles the real thing.

Preheat the oven to 400°F/200°C. Cut 2 of the eggplants in half lengthwise and place cut side up in a baking pan. Brush the exposed flesh with some of the olive oil. Roast them until caramelized and shrunken, 30 to 40 minutes.

Meanwhile, in a large skillet sauté the shallots and garlic in the remaining olive oil until the shallots are softened. Add the cinnamon and cook a few moments more. Remove the pan from the heat.

While the eggplant halves roast, grill the remaining 2 eggplants: Slice them in half lengthwise, place them cut side down and cut them lengthwise into long ½-inch/1 cm thick slices. Brush each slice with olive oil and season with salt and pepper. Grill each slice carefully, just cooking it through and forming characteristic grill marks on each side. (If you don't have a grill you may place the slices in a baking pan and bake them until just cooked, about 15 minutes.)

Remove the eggplant halves from the oven. Let cool, then remove the skins and finely chop the eggplant. Scrape the skins with a spoon if necessary to remove all of the flesh. Add the eggplant and the lemon zest and juice to the cinnamon mixture and cook, stirring frequently, until the eggplant thickens. Season with salt and pepper.

4 large eggplants

4 tablespoons / 60 mL extra virgin olive oil

2 shallots, minced

4 cloves garlic, minced

1 teaspoon / 5 mL cinnamon

Zest and juice of 1 lemon

Salt and pepper to taste

continued > >

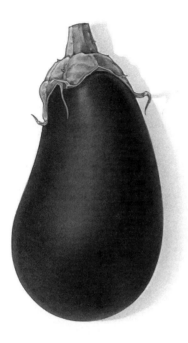

Lay the grilled eggplant slices into 4 ring molds about 3½ inches/9 cm wide by 1½ inches/4 cm tall. Overlap the slices in the center, and drape them up over the side of the mold. Fill with the cinnamon eggplant mixture. Fold the ends of the slices back over the filling, making sure the slices just overlap around the tart so that no filling spills out.

Serve immediately or reserve and reheat in a microwave when needed. To serve, invert the tart onto a small plate, slide a small thin spatula under the tart, and transfer it to the dinner plate, then gently remove the mold.

If the mixture is soupy and won't hold its shape in the mold, place it in a pot over a high heat and stir until it dries and thickens. Work neatly when overlapping the grilled eggplant so that none of the filling spills out.

Tomato Mint Sauce

2 tablespoons / 25 mL lamb fat or olive oil

2 shallots, minced

2 cloves garlic, minced

1 cup / 250 mL Cabernet Sauvignon

1 large very ripe tomato, diced

1 cup / 250 mL lamb glace, lamb broth, or rich beef stock

¼ cup / 60 mL thinly sliced mint (chiffonade)

Salt and pepper to taste

In a medium saucepan, sauté the shallots and garlic in the lamb fat until softened, 2 to 3 minutes. Add the wine and tomato and bring the mixture to a simmer. Continue simmering until the liquid reduces and thickens. Add the broth and return to a simmer for several minutes.

Purée the sauce in a blender, strain it through a fine-mesh strainer, and return it to the saucepan. Reserve until needed.

Shortly before serving, reheat the sauce and stir in the mint. Season with salt and pepper and serve immediately.

The mint's fragile flavor is lost if it is allowed to simmer, which is why it's added last. You may find that a rich broth is perfectly seasoned naturally and doesn't require added salt.

Tomato Parmesan–Crusted Rack of Lamb

Preheat the oven to 400°F/200°C.

Heat a large, heavy skillet over high heat. Place the racks meat side down in the skillet and sear until nicely browned, 3 to 5 minutes. Turn and brown the other side. Transfer them to a rack in a small roasting pan.

Whisk together the tomato paste, egg yolks, and half of the cheese. Spread the mixture evenly on the meat side of the racks. Process the bread and remaining cheese in a food processor until crumbly. Sprinkle evenly onto the paste mixture.

Roast the lamb until medium rare. A thermometer inserted in the center of the meat will register 125°F/50°C. Let rest covered with foil for 10 minutes. (Meanwhile, reheat the eggplant tarts and the tomato sauce.) Slice into chops between the bones and serve immediately.

The lamb is seared first to build flavor, and the crusting process insulates the meat a bit, so this is the only chance you get to properly caramelize the meat. Resting the meat for several minutes before cutting allows it to relax and reabsorb its agitated internal juices. If you slice it straight out of the oven, those juices and their flavor will be lost.

2 trimmed and frenched racks of lamb (1½ to 2 pounds / 750 g to 1 kg each), 8 bones each

¼ cup / 60 mL tomato paste

2 egg yolks

½ cup / 125 mL grated Parmesan cheese

1 cup / 250 mL cubed bread (about 2 slices)

The Plate!

Ladle ¼ cup/60 mL of the sauce into the center of each of 4 heated plates. Position an eggplant tart in the center of the sauce. Arrange the lamb chops around the tart. Garnish with a mint sprig or two. Serve with a baah!

Mint sprigs

Double Smoked Bacon Roast Tenderloin of Pork with Garlic Lentils, Mustard Sauce, and Apple Tarragon Relish

I often combine two similar ingredients such as pork loin and bacon in one cooking method. This is my all-time favorite way to roast pork loin. Its affinity for its neighbor, bacon, shines through in this method, and the accompanying flavors are a welcome addition.

◇ 4 SERVINGS ◇

TIMING: SMOKE THE PORK TENDERLOIN THE DAY BEFORE. | MAKE THE RELISH AND SAUCE A FEW HOURS AHEAD. | AS THE LENTILS SIMMER, ROAST THE PORK AND BAKE THE BACON.

Double Smoked Bacon Roast Tenderloin of Pork

2 pork tenderloins (about 1 pound / 500 g each)

6 slices smoked bacon, at room temperature

Pepper

4 raw spaghetti noodles

Trim each tenderloin into 2 uniform pieces each about 5 to 6 ounces/140 to 175 g. Cut off the tapered end and remove the membrane on the other end. Each piece should be about 4 inches/10 cm long. Reserve the trimmed-off parts for another use.

Cut each bacon slice in half. Lay 3 half slices of bacon next to each other, slightly overlapping them along their long edges. Season the bacon liberally with pepper.

Lay 1 of the pork tenderloins sideways along the end of the bacon slices. Roll the pork in the bacon, stretching the bacon tightly. Thread the raw spaghetti through the overlapping ends of the bacon slices to secure them. Break off any overhanging ends of the spaghetti.

Chill the pork for 60 minutes. The pork may be made to this point the day before.

Preheat the oven to 400°F/200°C. Place the pork on a rack in a roasting pan. Roast the pork until the bacon crisps and the meat registers 145°F/165°C on a meat thermometer, 15 to 20 minutes. Remove the meat from the oven and let stand for 5 minutes in a warm place.

The bacon should go around the meat only once and overlap just enough to be secured with the spaghetti. If the bacon is too long, trim it. The spaghetti will dissolve during the cooking. Chilling the roasts well before they go in the oven gives the bacon extra time to crisp before the heat penetrates to the center of the meat.

Apple Tarragon Relish

Whisk together the oil, vinegar, mustard, and tarragon. Season with salt and pepper. Add the apple and onion, and toss to combine. Serve immediately or within a few hours.

A crisp apple such as a Granny Smith or McIntosh works best in this relish. Toss the relish frequently to keep the ingredients well combined as they rest and blend.

4 tablespoons / 60 mL extra virgin olive oil

4 tablespoons / 60 mL cider vinegar

1 tablespoon / 15 mL whole grain mustard

1 tablespoon / 15 mL minced tarragon

Salt and pepper to taste

1 apple, julienned

½ red onion, thinly sliced

Bacon Batons

Preheat the oven to 350°F/180°C.

Cut the bacon lengthwise into thin pieces. Sandwich the bacon between two pieces of parchment paper. Lay the paper on a baking stone or ovenproof floor tile and top with a second baking stone.

Bake the bacon until crisp, 15 to 20 minutes.

4 slices bacon

Whole Grain Mustard Sauce

6 slices bacon, chopped

½ cup / 125 mL water

1 cup / 250 mL chopped onion

2 cloves garlic, minced

2 cups / 500 mL pork or chicken broth

½ cup / 125 mL whole grain mustard

Salt and pepper to taste

Place the bacon and water in a heavy saucepan over medium heat and bring the mixture to a simmer. Continue simmering as the bacon releases its fat and the water boils off. Stir frequently as the bacon begins to brown. When it is crisp carefully pour off half of the fat and add the onion.

Cook the onion for a few minutes, stirring, until it is golden. Add the garlic and stir for a few minutes longer until you can smell its fragrance.

Add the broth and mustard. Bring the mixture to a simmer and continue cooking, stirring occasionally, until the onion is soft and the liquid is reduced by a third.

Purée the sauce until smooth in a blender. Return it to the saucepan, season it with salt and pepper, and reserve.

When ready to serve, gently reheat the sauce.

For a rustic variation, strain out the browned bacon, then continue making the sauce. Add the crisp bacon after puréeing and straining the sauce. The little pieces of bacon are a nice addition.

Garlic Lentils

1 cup / 250 mL French green lentils

6 slices bacon, chopped

2½ cups / 625 mL water

1 cup / 250 mL chopped onion

4 cloves garlic, minced

Pick over the lentils and discard any stones.

Place the bacon and ½ cup/125 mL of the water in a heavy saucepan over medium heat and bring the mixture to a simmer. Continue simmering as the bacon releases its fat and the water boils off. Stir frequently as the bacon begins to brown. When it is crisp carefully pour off half of the fat and add the onion.

Tomato Parmesan–Crusted Rack of Lamb
with Tomato Mint Sauce and a Cinnamon
Eggplant "Caviar" Tart
(page 115)

Double Smoked Bacon Roast Tenderloin of Pork
with Garlic Lentils, Mustard Sauce,
and Apple Tarragon Relish
(page 118)

Butterscotch-Glazed Apples and Yogurt
Cheese in a Crisp Leaf with an Apple Fritter
and Calvados Cider Sauce
(page 161)

A Time for Chocolate: Chocolate Coconut Clock Tower
with Cookie Clock Hands,
Roast Pineapple Vanilla Sauce,
and the Correct Time
(page 173)

Cook the onion for a few minutes, stirring, until it is golden. Add the garlic and stir for a few minutes longer until you can smell it.

Add the lentils, bay leaf, and remaining 2 cups/500 mL water. Bring the mixture to a simmer. Cover, reduce the heat, and continue cooking at a bare simmer until the lentils are nearly done, about 20 minutes.

Add the carrot and garlic scapes, stirring just to combine, and continue simmering the lentils for another few minutes until they are just done. Discard the bay leaf. Season with salt and pepper. Serve immediately.

1 bay leaf

1 cup / 250 mL finely chopped carrot

½ cup / 125 mL finely sliced garlic scapes*

Salt and pepper to taste

*IF GARLIC SCAPES (SOMETIMES KNOWN AS SHOOTS) ARE UNAVAILABLE, USE 2 MORE CLOVES OF GARLIC AT THE BEGINNING OF THE RECIPE AND STIR IN ½ CUP / 125 ML SLICED GREEN ONION OR MINCED CHIVES AT THE END.

French green lentils are my favorite variety. They have an intense earthy flavor and retain their shape well when cooked.

The Plate!

Spoon about ¼ cup/60 mL of the sauce onto each of 4 hot plates. Top with a large spoonful of the lentils. Slice the pork into medallions and arrange on top of the lentils. Top with a handful of the apple relish. Garnish with a sprig of tarragon and 2 bacon batons. Serve with a grin!

Tarragon sprigs

◈ TARRAGON ◈

The first herb gardener I ever met was a wise old woman who had served as a senior cook in one of the first kitchens where I apprenticed. She ran circles around me and kept an herb garden behind the hotel. She taught me that the best tarragon was grown only from cuttings, not seeds. Tarragon's sharp pungent flavor always reminds me of her sunny garden and its effect on my growing understanding of cuisine.

Fennel Roast Striploin
with Shortrib Tarragon Ravioli,
Sherry Vinegar Onion Jam, and Sherry Broth

Making pasta is very easy but it does require time and patience. Since you're hauling out all the gear you might as well try something interesting like the herb inlay in the ravioli sheets used here. It's a perfect way to show off the tasty filling and complement the rich flavors of the beef.

◇ 6 TO 8 SERVINGS ◇

TIMING: MAKE THE JAM UP TO A WEEK AHEAD. | BRAISE THE SHORTRIBS THE DAY BEFORE. | MAKE THE PASTA DOUGH
SEVERAL HOURS OR A DAY AHEAD. | SEVERAL HOURS IN ADVANCE PREPARE THE RAVIOLIS.
| AT THE LAST MINUTE COOK THE MEAT AND RAVIOLIS AND REHEAT THE JAM AND BROTH.

Sherry Vinegar Onion Jam

2 tablespoons / 25 mL sugar

2 tablespoons / 25 mL water

1 large onion, sliced

¼ cup / 60 mL sherry vinegar

¼ cup / 60 mL snipped chives

Salt and pepper to taste

Melt the sugar and water together in a small, heavy saucepan over low heat. Increase the heat and simmer the syrup as the water evaporates and the sugar rises in temperature. Swirl it gently as it begins to color. When it is a deep golden brown, add the onion and vinegar; the caramel will bubble.

Continue simmering, stirring frequently, as the onions release their moisture and the vinegar and water reduce. Reduce the heat as needed to prevent the mixture from sticking and burning. When the onions have thickened to a jam-like consistency, remove them from the heat. This will take at least 30 minutes.

Season the jam with salt and pepper. The jam may be made well in advance. Store it covered and refrigerated. Reheat it before serving and stir in the chives at the last second.

The caramel forms a rich base for the jam and its assertive flavors. The chives are added last and not heated, so their delicate, pungent flavor and color are preserved.

Braised Shortrib Ravioli Filling and Sherry Broth

Heat the fat in a large Dutch oven or high-sided pot. Add the ribs in batches and brown them until they are evenly browned all over. Don't crowd the pan. Remove the ribs as they are browned. Pour off most of the fat.

Add the onion, celery, and carrot and sauté until they just begin to color. Add the garlic and cook a moment longer. Return the ribs to the pot, nestling them into the vegetables. Add the stock, sherry, and bay leaves and bring to a simmer.

Simmer 3 hours, covered tightly. (You may also bake them in a 300°F/150°C oven for that time.)

Remove the ribs and reserve. Strain and refrigerate the broth until the fat solidifies on the surface. This will take several hours or even overnight. Skim the fat off the broth and discard the fat, then reduce the broth to 2 cups/500 mL. Season the broth with salt and pepper.

When the ribs have cooled, remove the bones and discard. Place the meat in a food processor with the Parmesan and tarragon. Process until smooth. Taste and season. Reserve the ravioli filling, refrigerated, until needed.

2 tablespoons / 25 mL rendered beef fat or vegetable oil

3 pounds / 1.5 kg beef shortribs, excess fat trimmed, cut into 3-inch / 8 cm pieces

1 cup / 250 mL chopped onion

1 cup / 250 mL chopped celery

1 cup / 250 mL chopped carrot

4 large cloves garlic, minced

4 cups / 1 L rich beef stock

2 cups / 500 mL dry sherry

3 bay leaves

Salt and pepper to taste

½ cup / 125 mL grated Parmesan cheese

2 tablespoons / 25 mL fresh tarragon leaves

Take your time braising the ribs. The meat is very tough but you will be rewarded with a richly flavored filling if you're patient. Don't use pre-grated canned Parmesan; its pale flavors are disrespectful to the rich beef!

Ravioli Pasta

1 cup / 250 mL semolina flour, plus more for flouring

2 cups / 500 mL all-purpose flour

5 eggs, lightly beaten

½ cup / 125 mL fresh tarragon leaves

Place the flours and the eggs in the bowl of a standing mixer fitted with the dough hook and knead until smooth. Add a tablespoon or two of water if necessary to bring the dough together. On a lightly floured surface, knead the dough by hand for a few minutes. Let the dough rest, covered, for half an hour or longer. It may rest overnight.

Either roll the pasta out by hand with a rolling pin, which will take patience, or use a machine, following the manufacturer's instructions. Roll the pasta into a long elastic rectangular sheet ¹⁄₁₆ of an inch/1 mm thick. Use lots of semolina to keep the dough from sticking to you, the work surface, or the tools.

Sprinkle the tarragon leaves on one half of the pasta, evenly distributing them. Fold over the other half. Pass the dough through the machine once more, or use a rolling pin, to spread out the leaves.

Using a 4-inch/10 cm round cookie cutter, cut 18 to 24 circles from the pasta. Sprinkle each piece with semolina to prevent sticking and reserve in an airtight container in the refrigerator until needed.

Kneading the dough stresses it out, so by giving it time to relax you can make it much easier to roll out and work with. When you sprinkle on the herb leaves don't overlap them or they will weaken the dough when it is rolled further. Any leafy herb works well in this method.

Raviolis

Place a heaping tablespoon of the filling in the center of each pasta circle. Moisten your fingers with water and rub the pasta vigorously until it feels sticky. Top with another pasta circle. Gently press out any air and crimp in a ravioli clamp or with a fork along the edges of the circle.

Sprinkle the ravioli with semolina and reserve until needed.

Bring a large pot of salted water to a simmer and cook the raviolis for 5 to 7 minutes, or until the pasta is slightly soft (al dente) and the filling is heated through. Serve immediately.

Reserved ravioli filling

Reserved pasta circles

Fennel Roast Striploin

Press the fennel seed into the top of each steak.

In a medium nonstick skillet, melt the butter over medium-high heat. Add the steaks, fennel side down, and brown them evenly, turning them once. As they cook baste them with the hot pan juices. Judge the meat's doneness with your fingers by prodding it; when it feels firm, proceed. It will take 10 to 15 minutes to cook to medium rare. (Meanwhile, reheat the broth and cook the raviolis.)

Let the meat rest briefly on a rack. Pour off most of the fat in the pan. Add the sherry and reduce it to a glaze over high heat, stirring to dislodge any particles in the pan. Slice the meat and serve immediately.

4 (6-ounce / 175 g) striploin steaks, trimmed of fat and sinew

¼ cup / 60 mL coarsely ground fennel seed

4 tablespoons / 60 mL butter

¼ cup / 60 mL dry sherry

Resting the meat for several minutes before cutting allows it to relax and reabsorb its agitated internal juices. If you slice it straight out of the oven, those juices and their flavor will be lost. If the sherry glaze looks "broken," add a few tablespoons of cream and reduce quickly, stirring until it's smooth.

The Plate!

Tarragon sprigs

Chives

Arrange 3 raviolis in each of 6 to 8 heated broad, shallow bowls. Ladle in about ½ cup/125 mL of the broth. Fan out slices of the beef in the center. Drizzle the reserved sherry glaze over the meat. Add a dollop of the jam on the beef and garnish with a tarragon sprig and a few chives. Serve with a moo!

❖ SHERRY ❖

Authentic sherry is made only in sunny southwestern Spain from the Palomino and Pedro Ximenez grapes. After fermentation it is fortified with brandy, then stored in wooden casks where it oxidizes and concentrates, losing 3 percent of its volume a year "to the angels," as the locals claim. In the Solera barrel system, as it ages it is blended with other years, resulting in a non-vintage wine that ranges from the dry Manzanilla and Fino, to Amontillado, then Oloroso, and finally the sweet Cream.

Roasted Maple-Cured Back Bacon
with Sage Walnut Pesto, Bacon Onion Broth,
and Bacon White Bean Cake

Curing meat used to be a necessary cook's skill before the advent of refrigeration.
Now it's a great way to flavor meat. This method reflects its historical origins and updates them
with a long flavorful curing time for the pork. The presentation is completed with the
addition of mellow beans, pungent sage, and hearty walnuts.

◇ 4 SERVINGS ◇

TIMING: CURE THE LOIN 7 DAYS IN ADVANCE. | MAKE AND FREEZE THE BROTH UNTIL NEEDED. | THE PESTO CAN BE MADE SEVERAL DAYS AHEAD.
| SOAK THE BEANS OVERNIGHT, THEN FINISH THE BEAN CAKES AND THE BACON BROTH AS THE LOIN ROASTS.

Pork Loin and Its Broth

Preheat the oven to 400°F/200°C.

Remove the tenderloin from the loin and reserve for another use. Cut away the pork loin from the bone. Trim off most of the fat cap, leaving ¼ inch/5 mm. Cut off the irregularly shaped ham end just past the hip cartilage and reserve for another use. Reserve the trimmed loin for curing.

Chop the bones and place with the trimmings in a roasting pan with about ½ inch/1 cm of water. Roast until the bones are golden brown, about 60 minutes. The water will protect the pan from burning as the pork juices are released; ideally it will finish evaporating near the end of the roasting time and allow the meat juices to caramelize as well.

Transfer the bones to a stockpot. Pour the wine into the roasting pan and stir to dislodge and dissolve any remaining particles. Simmer briefly if needed or let rest for 15 minutes to fully dissolve any lingering essence. Add to the pot with the bones.

1 bone-in pork loin (about 4 pounds / 2 kg)*

2 cups / 500 mL Cabernet Sauvignon

4 onions, chopped

4 large carrots, chopped

4 stalks celery, chopped

4 bay leaves

*INSTEAD OF BUTCHERING THE PORK LOIN YOURSELF, ASK YOUR BUTCHER TO TRIM THE LOIN AND INCLUDE THE CUT-UP BONES AND TRIMMINGS.

continued > >

Add the vegetables and bay leaves. Add enough water to just cover all of the ingredients. Bring the mixture to a simmer, and simmer, uncovered, for 3 to 5 hours. Add more water to ensure that the ingredients are always covered. Cook until the broth is very flavorful and any scraps of meat are bland and flavorless.

Strain the broth through a fine strainer into a clean pot. Refrigerate then freeze the broth, allowing the fat to congeal at the top. Remove the solidified fat and discard. Reserve the broth until needed.

Maple-Cured Back Bacon

1 ½ cups / 375 mL coarse sea salt

¼ cup / 60 mL salt-peter

1 quart / 1 L maple syrup

2 quarts / 2 L water

Reserved trimmed pork loin

In a stockpot, heat the sea salt, salt-peter, maple syrup, and water just until the salt is dissolved. Skim off and discard any froth. Pour the brine through a strainer into a clean metal storage container. Add the meat, cut into 2 or 3 pieces if needed to fit it in.

Cover the container and place it in the refrigerator. Let rest for 1 week.

Preheat the oven to 350°F/180°C.

Remove the meat from the brine. Place it on a rack in a roasting pan and roast it until a meat thermometer placed in the thickest part of the meat registers 140 to 145°F/60 to 65°C. This will take about 45 minutes. Let the pork rest, covered with foil, for 15 minutes before serving. (During the rest the meat will relax and retain its juices; it will also rise in temperature about 5°F/2°C.) Reheat the bacon broth and sear the bean cakes while the pork is resting.

Make sure the meat is submerged in the brine, and weight it down if necessary. The salt-peter helps to preserve the color of the meat that would be lost in the curing process.

Bacon White Bean Cake

Soak the beans overnight in enough water to cover. Drain them.

Place the bacon in a medium saucepan over medium heat and cook until it is crisp and has rendered its fat. Add the onions and garlic and continue cooking until the onions are softened. Add the beans and broth and bring to a simmer. Simmer, covered, until the beans are tender and have absorbed all of the liquid, about 30 minutes.

Place half of the beans and the egg in a food processor and process until smooth. Return the puréed beans to the saucepan. Add the chives and stir just to combine.

Pat the mixture into 4 cakes 3 inches/8 cm wide and reserve on a plate.

Just before serving, heat some oil in a medium nonstick skillet over medium heat and sear the bean cakes.

Be sure the beans are fully cooked and not too moist or they won't hold together. If your mixture is too moist, add some bread crumbs to strengthen it.

1 cup / 250 mL dried white beans

4 ounces / 125 g bacon, chopped

1 cup / 250 mL minced onions

4 cloves garlic, minced

2 cups / 500 mL pork or chicken broth

1 egg

¼ cup / 60 mL snipped chives

Oil for frying

Sage Walnut Pesto

Place all the ingredients in a food processor and process until almost smooth. Serve immediately or refrigerate for up to 3 days.

For added flavor, roast the walnuts before making the pesto. The walnut oil is very flavorful and the key to the deep walnut flavor of the dish. Refrigerate any leftover oil, as it can turn rancid very quickly.

1 cup / 250 mL walnut pieces

½ cup / 125 mL packed sage leaves

½ cup / 125 mL grated Parmesan cheese

2 cloves garlic

½ cup / 125 mL walnut oil

Salt and pepper to taste

Bacon Onion Broth

6 slices bacon, finely sliced

½ cup / 125 mL water

1 ½ cups / 375 mL minced onion

6 cloves garlic, minced

1 cup / 250 mL Marsala

2 cups / 500 mL reserved pork loin broth

1 teaspoon / 5 mL red wine vinegar

Salt and pepper to taste

Place the bacon and water in a medium, heavy saucepan and bring to a simmer over medium-high heat. Continue cooking as the water evaporates and the bacon renders its fat. When the water is evaporated and the bacon pieces are crisp and brown, add the onion. Continue cooking, stirring frequently, until the onions are browned. Add the garlic and cook a few minutes longer.

Add the Marsala, broth, and vinegar and simmer until the liquid is reduced by one-third. Season with salt and pepper, and reserve.

The water added to the raw bacon helps render it evenly before it begins to brown. Don't burn the brown bits on the bottom of the pot — they are the flavor base and will dissolve into the broth. You may also purée this broth, forming a sauce if you prefer.

The Plate!

Sage sprigs

Ladle ¼ cup/60 mL of the bacon onion broth into the center of each of 4 heated plates. Position a bean cake in the center of the plate. Thinly slice the back bacon and arrange it around the cake. Add a dollop of the pesto and garnish with a sage sprig. Serve with an oink!

◇ SAGE ◇

Sage is native to the chalky arid hillsides of the Mediterranean. After ancient Druids got hold of it they used it to raise the dead. Today the vast majority of the dried version sold in North America is used to flavor turkey stuffing. There are many distinctly flavorful versions of sage, which is a member of the mint family. It grows easily and flowers spectacularly. Its strong pungency is a welcome flavor.

Cabernet Sauvignon–Glazed Venison Loin with Toasted Barley Risotto, Asparagus, Roast Carrot and Balsamic Vinegar Sauce, and Carrot Horseradish Jam

Farm-raised venison is commonly available today and offers a tasty, distinct alternative to other meats. Its rich flavor requires hearty balancing flavors such as roast carrots, balsamic vinegar, barley, and asparagus. Venison is also much lower in fat and cholesterol than beef.

◇ 4 SERVINGS, WITH LEFTOVER JAM ◇

TIMING: MAKE THE SAUCE UP TO 1 DAY AHEAD. MAKE THE JAM UP TO 7 DAYS AHEAD. | BEGIN THE BARLEY RISOTTO. AS IT COOKS, ROAST THE VENISON. | STEAM THE ASPARAGUS JUST BEFORE SERVING.

Roast Carrot and Balsamic Vinegar Sauce

In a medium, heavy saucepan, heat the oil over high heat. Add the carrots and cook them, stirring frequently, until they are evenly caramelized. Lower the heat as necessary to prevent the carrots from burning.

Add the garlic and shallots and cook a few minutes longer. Add the broth and vinegar. Simmer gently, uncovered, for about 15 minutes, reducing the liquid slightly, until the carrots are very soft.

Pour the mixture into a blender and purée until the sauce is smooth. If the sauce is slightly too thick, add a bit of water to thin it. Strain it through a fine-mesh strainer and season with salt and pepper.

Reserve for up to 1 day, and reheat just before serving.

The key to this sauce's flavor is the roasting. The carrots will dry out a bit and toughen, but the simmering softens them so they purée well. Carrots vary; if the sauce is thin, simmer it gently to reduce and thicken it.

4 tablespoons / 60 mL extra virgin olive oil

2 cups / 500 mL chopped carrots

2 cloves garlic, minced

2 shallots, minced

3 cups / 750 mL venison broth (or rich chicken or veal stock)

½ cup / 125 mL balsamic vinegar

Salt and pepper to taste

Carrot Horseradish Jam

1 cup / 250 mL chopped carrot

1 cup / 250 mL water

1 tablespoon / 15 mL horseradish

¼ cup / 60 mL extra virgin olive oil

Salt

Place the carrot and water in a small saucepan and bring them to a gentle simmer. Cook the mixture until the carrots are soft and the water evaporates. Pour the mixture into a blender or food processor, add the horseradish and oil, and purée the jam. Taste and season. The jam may be stored, covered, up to 7 days in the refrigerator.

Toasted Barley Risotto

1 cup / 250 mL barley

4 to 6 cups / 1 to 1.5 L venison broth (or a rich chicken or veal stock)

2 tablespoons / 25 mL extra virgin olive oil

2 cups / 500 mL chopped onions

2 cloves garlic, minced

1 cup / 250 mL Cabernet Sauvignon

1 cup / 250 mL finely minced or shredded carrot

1 cup / 250 mL snipped chives

Salt and pepper to taste

Place the barley in a skillet large enough to hold it in one layer. Place the skillet on high heat and toast the barley, gently shivering the pan until the grains are an even deep golden brown. Remove from the heat.

Bring the broth to a simmer in a saucepan.

In a medium, heavy saucepan, heat the oil over high heat. Add the onions and sauté them until they are a deep even golden brown. Add the garlic and cook a minute or so longer.

Add the wine and reduce the heat to medium. Stir in the barley as the wine evaporates. When the barley is lightly glazed, add ¼ cup/60 mL of the broth. Stir frequently as the mixture simmers; reduce the heat to maintain a simmer. When the broth is absorbed, add ¼ cup/60 mL more. Continue stirring and adding broth until the barley is cooked, 30 to 40 minutes.

When the barley is cooked through but still retains its pleasing texture, stir in the carrots and cook a further few minutes. If you are serving the barley immediately, stir in the chives and season with salt and pepper. Or set the barley aside. Just before serving, stir in the chives and season it to taste.

Cabernet Sauvignon–Glazed Venison Loin

Preheat the oven to 400°F/200°C.

Cook the venison only when all of the preceding plate elements are done or nearly done and you are nearly ready to serve. Pat the venison pieces dry, and season them with pepper. In a medium, heavy nonstick skillet over high heat, melt the butter. Add the venison; don't overcrowd the pan. Sear the pieces until they have a nicely browned crust. Spoon the hot fat over the venison while it is pan-roasting. It will take 5 to 7 minutes for each side to brown.

Remove the meat from the pan and rest it on a rack, not a flat surface. Cover it loosely with foil and keep it warm. Alternatively, place the pan in the oven for a few minutes until a meat thermometer inserted in the thickest part of the loin reads 120 to 130°F/50 to 55°C.

Add the wine to the pan. Swirl it around the pan to dislodge any browned bits. Use a wooden spoon if necessary. When the wine has reduced and has formed a glaze with the butter, return the venison to the pan and turn each piece, coating them evenly in the glaze. Serve immediately.

1 (1½ pound / 750 g) venison loin, cut in 2 even pieces

Pepper

2 tablespoons / 25 mL butter

1 cup / 250 mL Cabernet Sauvignon

Salt to taste

Asparagus

24 spears asparagus

A few minutes before serving, steam the asparagus.

The Plate!

Chives

Spoon ½ cup/125 mL of the carrot sauce into the center of each of 4 hot plates. Add a serving of the barley to the center of the plate. Use a 3-inch/8 cm wide by 1 ½-inch/4 cm tall mold to shape the barley into a puck-shaped tight pile.

Place 3 spears of asparagus on 3 other spears in a criss-cross fashion on the barley. Slice a portion of the meat and arrange it on the asparagus spears. Top with a spoonful of the jam and garnish with a few chives. Serve with a yip!

> ### ❖ BARLEY ❖
>
> *Barley was cultivated in Neolithic times — more than 5,000 years BC. It was much loved by the Greeks and Romans and is frequently mentioned in the Bible. In 1543 it was exported to the New World, where it was promptly turned into whisky. Today it is one of the top grains on the globe, although half of the crop is fed to beef cattle and much of the rest is used to make beer.*

Pistachio-Stuffed Roast Quail
with Sweet Potato Dumplings,
Wild Chanterelle Broth, and Sage Chips

Quail are my favorite game bird, because their succulent flavor is easy to create with.
In this presentation the opulent pistachio plays a starring role with the elusive wild chanterelle.
Together they show off the wonderful richness of the quail.

◇ 4 SERVINGS ◇

TIMING: MAKE AND RESERVE THE DUMPLINGS. | STUFF THE QUAIL AND BEGIN THE BROTH.
AS IT FINISHES, ROAST THE QUAIL AND MAKE THE CHIPS. | AT THE LAST SECOND, BROWN THE DUMPLINGS.

Sweet Potato Dumplings

Preheat the oven to 350°F/180°C. Pierce the potato with a fork several times and bake it for 60 minutes, until it shrinks noticeably and is tender.

Cut the potato in half and scoop the roasted pulp into a food processor fitted with a plastic dough blade. Add the egg and process to blend. Season with the salt and pepper.

Gradually add the flour, processing the mixture as it first resembles a batter and then just until a smooth ball of dough forms.

Lightly flour your work surface and turn out the ball of dough. Knead it a few times to make it easier to work with. Sprinkle the dough with enough flour to keep it from sticking. Divide it into 4 pieces and roll them out into cylinders 1 inch/2.5 cm thick. Cut each cylinder into inch-long dumplings.

Bring a large pot of salted water to a simmer. Add the dumplings and cook them for 5 to 7 minutes just to set the dough and cook it through. Remove them with a slotted spoon and let them dry briefly. Toss them in a little oil if not using them immediately. The dumplings may be made to this point and refrigerated overnight.

1 sweet potato

1 egg

Salt and pepper to taste

2 to 3 cups / 500 to 750 mL all-purpose flour

continued >>

When you are ready to serve the dumplings, reheat them by crisping them in butter in a nonstick skillet.

The more water that evaporates from the potato as it bakes, the less flour you will need to add to make a dough. Let it bake longer and your dumplings will be more flavorful. Try flavoring the dough with your favorite herb or spice. When the dough feels strong enough to roll out, stop adding flour to it.

Pistachio-Stuffed Roast Quail

8 slices bacon

4 ounces / 125 g boneless chicken breast

½ cup / 125 mL chopped chives

½ teaspoon / 2 mL salt

½ teaspoon / 2 mL pepper

½ cup / 125 mL toasted pistachios

4 semi-boneless quail

Note: If you are unable to find semi-boneless quail, buy bone-in quail and remove the bones yourself. Remove the breast bone, the ribcage, and the first leg bone. Cut off the wishbone and cut through the backbone if necessary. Gently and carefully run your fingers along the bones to separate them from the flesh. Reserve the bones for use in the chanterelle broth.

Preheat the oven to 400°F/200°C.

Chop 4 slices of the bacon. In a medium skillet over medium heat, brown the chopped bacon until crisp, turning the pieces during cooking. Discard half of the rendered fat.

In a food processor, process the chicken, the chives, and the crisp bacon and fat until smooth. Season the mixture with the salt and pepper. Transfer it to a bowl and stir in the pistachios.

Stuff each quail with several spoonfuls of the pistachio mixture. Form each quail into a tight ball. Wrap each quail with a slice of the remaining bacon. Cover as much of each breast as possible by only slightly overlapping the bacon as it wraps several times around the quail. Tuck in the end of the bacon slice along the back of the quail.

In an ovenproof uncrowded skillet, roast the quail 20 to 30 minutes on their backs, until a thermometer inserted in the stuffing reads 160°F / 70°C. The bacon will brown nicely along the way. (Meanwhile, reheat the chanterelle broth and crisp the dumplings, if needed.)

Let rest for several minutes. As they rest, pour off most of the fat in the skillet and dissolve any browned bits with some of the chanterelle broth, then add to the broth. Slice each quail in half through the center of the breasts. Serve immediately.

Wild Chanterelle Broth

In a heavy saucepan over medium heat, melt the butter. Add the shallots and garlic and cook, stirring frequently, until the shallots are soft and translucent.

Add the sherry and simmer until it reduces by two-thirds. Add the chicken broth and the mushrooms. Gently simmer the broth for 30 minutes, reducing it by half.

The broth may be made in advance and reheated. Add the sage and season with salt and pepper just before serving.

The distinctive fruity aroma of the chanterelles is perfectly accented by the sherry in this broth. If you can't find chanterelles, use another mushroom such as morels or shiitake.

1 tablespoon / 15 mL butter

½ cup / 125 mL minced shallots

2 cloves garlic, minced

1 cup / 250 mL dry sherry

4 cups / 1 L rich chicken broth (fortified with the reserved quail bones and scraps)

2 ounces / 50 g dried chanterelles (or 2 cups / 500 mL fresh)

2 tablespoons / 25 mL thinly sliced sage

Salt and pepper to taste

Sage Chips

Peel the potato and, using a mandoline or similar cutting tool, very thinly slice it crosswise. (A knife will not cut thin enough.)

1 baking potato

Small sage leaves

Oil for frying

continued > >

Match two equal-sized slices together. Rub them vigorously together for a moment to draw out their starch as an adhesive. Insert a sage leaf between the slices and press them together.

In a heavy deep pot, heat 4 inches/10 cm of oil to 365°F/185°C. Fry the chips until crisp, 3 to 5 minutes. Drain on paper towels. The cooled chips may be stored in an airtight container for several hours.

The Plate!

Good-quality sharp Parmesan cheese

Ladle about ½ cup/125 mL of the chanterelle broth into each of 4 hot wide, shallow bowls. Add 3 or 4 dumplings. Shave some Parmesan over the works and top with 2 quail halves. Garnish with several sage chips. Serve with a crunch!

> ### ◇ CHANTERELLES ◇
>
> *Foraging for wild chanterelles is one of the most pleasurable experiences possible for a country chef. From afar they seem regal and inviting. Their luminescent golden presence against the green mossy forest floor is an inspiring sight. Chanterelle patches are often jealously guarded secrets, but I love to show off my sites to anyone I know. People always appreciate the experience of witnessing them in their natural state.*

Ale-Braised Chicken with Malt Glaze, Barley Sausage, Garlic Braised Tomato, and Tomato Oregano Compote

Because most beer is flavorless it is often overlooked as a valid ingredient in cuisine. But a good flavorful ale is perfect for braising. I recommend a hearty micro-brewery ale. Taste the beer warm; if it's pale and lifeless like most beers it won't contribute to the braise. Make sure you save some to toast the success of the dish!

◈ 2 SERVINGS ◈

TIMING: BEGIN THE CHICKEN 4 TO 6 HOURS AHEAD. | AS THE STOCK SIMMERS, MAKE THE SAUSAGES, AND COOK THEM WHILE THE LEGS ARE BRAISING. | BEGIN BRAISING THE TOMATOES BEFORE THE LEGS. | WHILE THE TOMATOES AND LEGS BRAISE, MAKE THE COMPOTE. | WHEN THE LEGS AND TOMATOES ARE NEARLY DONE, ROAST THE BREAST.

Ale-Braised Chicken

Preheat the oven to 400°F/200°C. Thoroughly rinse the chicken under cold running water. Cut the legs off the chicken. Trim off any overhanging skin from the legs. Cut the breasts from the chicken and bone them, keeping the skin on; reserve the breasts and legs, covered and refrigerated.

Break the chicken carcass into smaller pieces and place the carcass, wings, and scraps in a small roasting pan or skillet. Pour about 2 cups/500 mL water into the pan to prevent it from burning. Roast the bones until they are golden brown, 45 to 60 minutes. Check every 20 minutes to be sure that the pan is not burning as the water evaporates, and add a little more water if necessary. Ideally the juices will caramelize as the bones finish roasting.

Place the contents of the roasting pan into a medium stockpot. Scrape the bottom of the roasting pan and, if necessary, add some water to the pan to dissolve any lingering particles. Cover the bones completely with water and simmer for 2 hours. Skim off and discard any fat or scum. Strain through a fine-mesh strainer into a saucepan and bring to a boil. Reduce to 2 cups/500 mL; reserve.

1 (3½-pound / 1.75 kg) chicken

4 tablespoons / 60 mL butter

1 cup / 250 mL chopped onion

1 cup / 250 mL chopped carrot

1 cup / 250 mL chopped celery

1 bottle flavorful ale

4 large oregano sprigs or branches

4 cloves garlic

2 bay leaves

Salt and pepper to taste

continued >>

In a medium, heavy saucepan over medium heat, melt the butter. Add the chicken legs and cook until golden brown on all sides. Remove the legs.

Add the onion, carrot, and celery to the butter and stir for a minute or two. Return the legs to the pot and add the ale, oregano, garlic, and bay leaves. Add the reserved broth. Bring the liquid to a bare simmer, cover the pot with a tight-fitting lid, and braise the chicken legs until a fork inserted into the legs meets no resistance, 60 to 90 minutes. Keep the broth at just barely a simmer.

Remove the legs from the broth with a slotted spoon. Using your fingers and a thin, sharp knife, carefully coax out the three bones, two in the leg and a third in the thigh. Be sure to remove any knuckle cartilage that may be left behind. Serve immediately or let rest in the hot broth until needed. Season the legs just before serving.

In braising you get only one chance — the initial searing — to build caramelized flavors before the liquids are added. The meat should barely simmer for best results.

Barley Sausage

1 (6-ounce / 175 g) chicken breast with skin, diced (the first reserved chicken breast)

1 cup / 250 mL cooked barley

½ cup / 125 mL grated Parmesan cheese

½ cup / 125 mL oregano leaves

Salt and pepper

Bring a large pot of water to a simmer. Meanwhile, in a food processor, process all the ingredients until almost smooth — the barley should still be slightly lumpy.

Place the mixture in a piping bag fitted with a ½-inch/1 cm plain tip. Spread a large sheet of plastic wrap on a lightly moistened work surface. Pipe the sausage filling along a long edge of the plastic, leaving a 2-inch/5 cm border, and leaving 1 inch/2.5 cm clear at each end of the sausage. Roll up the plastic wrap carefully: trying to avoid catching any air bubbles inside the plastic. Grasp both ends of the plastic wrap and twirl the works repeatedly until the plastic tightens around the sausage. Prick any air pockets with a pin. Tie both ends of the plastic with string, then tie the sausage at regular intervals, forming at least 4 links.

Poach the plastic-wrapped links in the simmering water until just cooked through, 5 to 7 minutes, depending on their thickness. Cool the sausages.

Cut off the plastic wrap and squeeze out the sausages. Just before serving, melt 1 tablespoon/15 mL butter in a nonstick skillet over medium heat. Add the sausages and heat them through, browning them slightly. Serve immediately.

Puréed chicken breast is very strong when it cooks, and it can bind a lot of other ingredients together. But make sure the barley is cooked and dry, not soupy, or it may overwhelm the chicken's strengthening abilities.

Garlic Braised Tomato

Preheat the oven to 300°F/150°C.

Slice the tomatoes in half crosswise. Place them face down in a small baking dish that they just fit in. Scatter the onion, garlic, oregano, and bay leaves over them. Add enough olive oil to just cover the tomatoes.

Cover the pan with foil and bake for 2 hours, until the tomatoes are softened and flavorful. Let the tomatoes rest for 20 minutes.

When you are ready to serve, carefully remove the tomato halves from the oil and drain them on a plate for a moment. Gently remove the skins. Serve the tomatoes immediately.

2 medium tomatoes

1 cup / 250 mL sliced onion

8 cloves garlic

Several large sprigs of oregano

2 bay leaves

Extra virgin olive oil

This method depends on a very fruity and flavorful olive oil for maximum flavor; regular oil won't flavor the tomatoes. Strain the remaining olive oil and reserve it for use in a complementary recipe that calls for olive oil. Meatier tomato varieties work best, but whatever type you use, make sure they're ripe!

Malt-Glazed Chicken

1 tablespoon / 15 mL olive oil

1 (6-ounce / 175 g) chicken breast with skin (the second reserved chicken breast)

½ cup / 125 mL barley malt extract

1 tablespoon / 15 mL Tabasco® pepper sauce

Salt

Preheat the oven to 400°F/200°C.

In a small ovenproof skillet over high heat, heat the oil. Add the chicken breast skin side down and sear it. Turn it when the bottom is golden brown and continue to cook until the other side is golden brown.

While the breast is searing, stir together the malt and Tabasco® in a shallow dish. Dip the seared chicken breast into the malt mixture, thoroughly coating it.

Return the chicken to the skillet and bake it just long enough to set the glaze and finish cooking the chicken, 5 to 10 minutes. Sprinkle with salt. Slice and serve immediately.

You may substitute molasses for the malt extract.

Tomato Oregano Compote

1 cup / 250 mL quartered cherry tomatoes

½ cup / 125 mL chopped oregano

2 tablespoons / 25 mL minced red onion

1 tablespoon / 15 mL red wine vinegar

1 tablespoon / 15 mL extra virgin olive oil

Salt and pepper to taste

In a medium bowl, toss all the ingredients together until thoroughly mixed. Let rest 30 minutes, then serve.

The Plate!

Place a deboned chicken leg in the center of each of 2 hot plates. Arrange 2 braised tomato halves and 2 of the sausages on each plate. Add a piece of sliced chicken breast and top it with a spoonful of the tomato compote. Garnish with an oregano sprig and just moisten each plate with ¼ cup/60 mL of the chicken braising liquid. Serve with a cackle!

Oregano sprigs

◇ OLIVE OIL ◇

Olives grow on trees that can be hundreds of years old and tolerate six months with no rain. They are picked green in September, in November when they are a ripe black, and in January when they are bursting with oil. That oil when first pressed is of the highest extra virgin grade. Later pressings introduce heat, which alters the oil and its fruity, peppery pungency. The most common grade is pumace, or plain, "Olive Oil" — it's a pale cousin to the premier varieties that precede it.

Goat Cheese–Stuffed Chicken Breast with Roast Garlic Broth and a Salad of Arugula and Grilled Red Onions

Good cooking is all about fully realizing the flavor potential of your ingredients. In this dish, every part of the chicken comes together to build a memorable flavor palette. The recipe is actually very simple, and when the goat cheese, roast garlic, and arugula kick in, the results are spectacular.

 2 SERVINGS

TIMING: MAKE THE BROTH THE DAY BEFORE OR 6 HOURS IN ADVANCE. | WHILE THE BROTH SIMMERS, STUFF THE BREASTS. | AS THE BROTH FINISHES, ROAST THE BREASTS AND MAKE THE SALAD.

Roast Garlic Broth

1 (3½-pound / 1.75 kg) chicken
2 heads garlic
1 cup / 250 mL white wine
1 large carrot, chopped
1 stalk celery, chopped
1 large onion, chopped
3 bay leaves
Salt and pepper to taste

Preheat the oven to 400°F/200°C.

Thoroughly rinse the chicken under cold running water. Cut off the last 2 sections of each wing, leaving the third section (wing drumstick) attached to the carcass. Cut the legs from the chicken. Trim the meat off the thighs and set aside. Place the drumsticks and thigh bones in a roasting pan. Remove the breasts, leaving the first joint of the wing bone attached to each breast. Remove the skin from the breasts by gently pulling it loose and over the end of the wing bone. Reserve the breasts and the thigh meat for the stuffing, covered and refrigerated.

Add all the scraps and the carcass to the roasting pan. Pour about 2 cups/ 500 mL water into the pan to prevent it from burning. Roast the bones until they are golden brown, 45 to 60 minutes. Check every 20 minutes to be sure that the pan is not burning as the water evaporates, and add a little more water if necessary. Ideally the juices will caramelize as the bones finish roasting.

Meanwhile, place the garlic heads in a small pan and roast alongside the bones until they begin to bubble through the top, about 60 minutes. Let cool to room temperature.

Transfer the roasted bones and scraps to a stockpot. Place the roasting pan over medium heat. Pour the wine into the roasting pan and stir to scrape up any browned bits. Pour some water into the roasting pan and stir it around. Pour the deglazing liquid into the stockpot.

Add the carrot, celery, onion, and bay leaves. Pour enough water into the pot to just cover the ingredients. Bring the broth to a simmer, cover, and simmer for 2 to 3 hours. Occasionally skim off and discard any fat or scum that rises to the top.

Strain the broth through a fine-mesh strainer into a saucepan and bring it to a boil. Reduce the broth to about 2 cups/500 mL, skimming as needed along the way.

Meanwhile, using a serrated knife, trim off the top of the garlic heads to expose the cloves and carefully squeeze out the roasted garlic.

Place the broth in a blender with the roasted garlic and purée it thoroughly. Season it to taste with salt and pepper, and chill it if you are not using it the same day.

Reheat the broth while you are baking the chicken breasts.

Roasting the chicken bones adds amazing character to what is often one-dimensional broth. Adding water to the roasting pan preserves the precious drippings in the bottom, which might burn otherwise. But don't add too much or the drippings won't brown — it's a delicate balance! Roasting the garlic mellows its flavor dramatically, leaving it rich and smooth.

Goat Cheese–Stuffed Chicken Breast

Reserved chicken breasts

Reserved thigh meat

4 ounces / 125 g goat cheese

¼ cup / 60 mL snipped chives

½ teaspoon / 2 mL salt

¼ teaspoon / 1 mL pepper

2 eggs

1 cup / 250 mL all-purpose flour

1 cup / 250 mL fresh white bread crumbs

Remove the tenderloin from each breast and set aside. With a sharp, flexible boning knife, carefully cut a deep pocket in the side of each breast, keeping the opening small. Make the cavity as big as possible and try not to cut through the breast.

In a food processor, thoroughly combine the reserved thigh meat, the goat cheese, and the chives, forming a mousse. Season the mousse with the salt and pepper. Place the mousse in a heavy-duty resealable freezer bag. Cut a corner off the bag, forming a piping bag. Insert the corner deep into the chicken pocket and squeeze in the filling, completely filling the space.

Place the reserved tenderloins in between layers of plastic wrap and gently flatten them with a rolling pin. Carefully insert the tenderloins just inside the slit in the breasts, forming a patch over the opening. Refrigerate or even slightly freeze the breasts to firm them.

Preheat the oven to 350°F/180°C. In a shallow dish, whisk together the eggs. Have ready in 2 separate dishes the flour and the bread crumbs. Working with one breast at a time, dust the chicken in the flour. Dip in the egg, letting the excess drip off. Roll the chicken in the bread crumbs, coating it thoroughly. Place the chicken on a baking pan and bake for 30 to 40 minutes until a meat thermometer inserted into the thickest part of the chicken reads 160°F/70°C and the crust is golden brown. Let rest for 5 minutes before serving.

As you cut into the breast, watch the protruding portion of your blade. If it is angled you may be cutting through the outside of the breast. It is sometimes useful to work on the edge of a thick cutting board so your knuckles have room. If you don't like goat cheese, try boursin or brie instead.

Salad of Arugula and Grilled Red Onions

Thinly slice the onion into rings. Whisk together the oil, lemon juice, lemon zest, and salt and pepper. Toss the onions into the mixture, let rest 10 minutes, then toss again. Place them on a preheated grill, turning after a few minutes until they are heated through. (If you don't have a grill, mix the onions with the dressing the day before, tossing them frequently, and let them rest overnight.) Reserve the dressing.

Just before serving, toss the dressing with the onions and arugula.

1 red onion

¼ cup / 60 mL extra virgin olive oil

Zest and juice of 2 lemons

Salt and pepper to taste

2 handfuls of arugula (4 to 6 ounces / 125 to 175 g)

The Plate!

Pour about ½ cup/125 mL of the broth into each of 2 hot wide, shallow bowls. Add a pile of the salad. Slice each chicken breast into 3 pieces and fan out over the salad. Serve with a cockle-doodle-doo!

◇ ARUGULA ◇

Arugula, also known as rocket, is a sharply flavored leafy green. It traces its culinary origins to the sunny Mediterranean, where its role as "a seasoning leaf" first brought it prominence. During the eighties and early nineties it served as a kind of culinary trend marker: if it appeared on a menu you were sure to find yourself in the throes of nouvelle cuisine shortly thereafter. Fortunately its aggressive flavor has found a place in today's less excessive cooking and it remains a favorite of chefs everywhere.

Roast Pheasant Breast and Cabernet-Braised Pheasant Legs with Cabernet Truffle Whipped Potatoes, Braised Aromatic Vegetables, and Thyme Gravy

Special ingredients such as pheasant and truffle often suffer from overwrought cooking methods. Like any other good ingredients, they benefit from respect and restraint. This presentation shows the way to elegant simplicity.

 2 SERVINGS

TIMING: BUTCHER THE PHEASANT, MAKE THE BROTH, AND MARINATE THE BREAST THE DAY BEFORE OR AT LEAST 6 HOURS IN ADVANCE. | BRAISE THE LEGS 2 HOURS AHEAD. WHILE THEY COOK MAKE THE POTATOES. | MAKE THE GRAVY AND ROAST THE BREAST.

Roast Pheasant Breast

1 (2 to 3-pound / 1 to 1.5 kg) pheasant

4 tablespoons / 60 mL extra virgin olive oil

1 tablespoon / 15 mL minced thyme

1 tablespoon / 15 mL minced shallot

Pepper to taste

1 teaspoon / 5 mL minced garlic

Coarse sea salt to taste

Thoroughly rinse the pheasant under cold running water. Cut off the last 2 sections of each wing. Carefully cut away the breasts, keeping the skin on and leaving the first joint of the wing attached to each breast. Remove the legs by first snapping them out of the socket and then trimming them close to the carcass so as not to waste any flesh. Trim off any overhanging skin from the legs. Reserve the legs, carcass, and trimmings, covered and refrigerated.

In a small bowl, whisk together the oil, thyme, shallot, pepper, and garlic. As soon as the breasts are removed from the pheasant, rub them with the marinade. Let rest, covered and refrigerated, overnight, or while the broth simmers and reduces.

After the legs have braised, preheat the oven to 400°F/200°C.

When you are almost ready to serve, remove the breasts from the marinade and place them on a rack in a roasting pan. Roast the breasts until they are just cooked through and remain juicy, 12 to 15 minutes. Season with salt and serve immediately.

Pheasant and Its Broth

Preheat the oven to 400°F/200°C.

Place the carcass and trimmings in a roasting pan. Pour in about ½ inch/1 cm of water to prevent the pan from burning. Roast the bones until they are golden brown, about 60 minutes Check the pan near the end of the roasting time to make sure it isn't burning; add a splash of water if necessary. Ideally the juices will caramelize as the bones finish roasting.

Transfer the roasted bones to a stockpot. Pour the wine into the roasting pan and stir to dislodge and dissolve any bits in the pan. Simmer over medium heat if needed or let rest for 15 minutes to fully dissolve any lingering essence. Add the liquid to the stockpot.

Add the onion, carrot, celery, garlic, thyme, and bay leaves. Add the broth and enough water to just cover the ingredients. Bring the broth to the simmer, and simmer, uncovered, for 3 hours. Add water to keep all the ingredients covered throughout the cooking time.

Strain the broth through a fine-mesh strainer into a saucepan. Bring it to a boil over high heat and reduce the broth to 3 cups/750 mL. Reserve, chilled, if you are not using it the same day.

For added flavor use plain chicken stock instead of water to make this broth.

Reserved carcass and trimmings

1 cup / 250 mL Cabernet Sauvignon

1 large onion, diced

1 large carrot, diced

1 stalk celery, diced

6 cloves garlic, sliced

4 thyme sprigs

2 bay leaves

4 cups / 1 L chicken broth or water

Cabernet-Braised Pheasant Legs and Thyme Gravy

¼ pound / 125 g butter (½ cup / 125 mL)

Reserved pheasant legs

4 whole shallots, peeled

8 cloves garlic, peeled

3 cups / 750 mL reserved broth

1 cup / 250 mL Cabernet Sauvignon

4 sprigs thyme

4 tablespoons / 60 mL all-purpose flour

¼ cup / 60 mL sour cream

Salt and pepper to taste

Preheat the oven to 300°F/150°C. In a heavy saucepan over medium-high heat, melt the butter. When the butter begins to foam, add the legs and brown them evenly on all sides. Remove the pan from the heat, transfer the legs to a casserole dish just large enough to hold them, and discard half the butter from the pan. Push the shallots and garlic in around the legs. Add the broth, wine, and 3 of the thyme sprigs.

Cover the casserole with a tight-fitting lid or foil and braise in the oven until the legs are tender, about 60 minutes.

Meanwhile, return the pan to a medium heat. Stir the flour into the butter to form a smooth paste. Continue stirring until the roux begins to brown and has a nutty aroma, 6 to 8 minutes. Reserve.

Transfer the legs, shallots, and garlic to a plate and keep warm. Mince the leaves from the last thyme sprig.

Slowly add the broth to the roux, whisking it constantly, then stirring for 10 to 15 minutes over medium heat until it has thickened. Stir in the thyme leaves and sour cream. Season with salt and pepper, and serve immediately.

Cabernet Truffle Whipped Potatoes

2 large potatoes, peeled

1 cup / 250 mL Cabernet Sauvignon

1 cup / 250 mL heavy cream

1 ounce / 25 g shaved truffles

Salt and pepper to taste

Steam the potatoes until tender. Meanwhile, place the wine and cream in a small saucepan and reduce to ½ cup/125 mL.

Pass the potatoes through a food mill onto a baking sheet. Dry the potatoes in a 300 or 400°F/150 or 200°C oven for several minutes. Place the potatoes in a heavy saucepan and briskly beat in the cream reduction. Keep the potatoes warm for up to 30 minutes.

At the last second stir in the truffles, season with salt and pepper, and serve immediately.

If you can find them, Yukon gold potatoes are best for this purée, for they are richly flavored and creamy when cooked.

The Plate!

Place a neat pile of the potatoes in the center of each of 2 heated plates. Ladle ¼ cup/60 mL of the gravy around the potatoes. Add a braised pheasant leg. Slice the breasts and fan them out on the plates. Top with the braised shallots and garlic. Garnish with a thyme sprig. Serve with a swoop!

Thyme sprigs

◆ TRUFFLES ◆

Truffles are perhaps the most luxurious of all ingredients. Their rich, earthy flavor was thought to be the result of lightning hitting the spot where they were found growing. They have never been successfully cultivated and are found only in France, Italy, and sometimes Spain, although rumor has it that the Chinese are hoarding a variety. They grow underground amidst the roots of oak trees and can be found only by specially trained dogs and pigs.

Roast Garlic–Stuffed Squab
with Wild Rice Almond Pudding,
Ground-Cherry Chutney, and Sage Jus

When I was a kid I wouldn't go near chicken livers, so it's quite an evolution for me to voluntarily cook with them now. Their richness makes this stuffing memorable, highlighting the juicy tenderness of the squab. My mom would be proud!

◇ 4 SERVINGS ◇

TIMING: DEBONE THE SQUAB AND MAKE THE JUS THE DAY BEFORE OR SEVERAL HOURS AHEAD. | STUFF THE SQUAB AND MAKE THE CHUTNEY. | BAKE THE PUDDINGS AND STUFFED SQUAB TOGETHER.

Sage Jus

2 (1-pound / 500 g) squab

1 cup / 250 mL Cabernet Sauvignon

4 cups / 1 L chicken broth

2 bay leaves

1 cup / 250 mL chopped onion

1 cup / 250 mL chopped carrot

1 cup / 250 mL chopped celery

Salt and pepper to taste

1 tablespoon / 15 mL thinly sliced sage leaves

Preheat the oven to 400°F/200°C.

Debone the squab: Remove the breast bone, the ribcage, and the first leg bone. Cut off the wishbone and cut through the backbone if necessary. Gently and carefully run your fingers along the bones to separate them from the flesh. Reserve the semi-boneless squab.

Place the squab bones in a small roasting pan or skillet, and roast until golden brown, 30 to 45 minutes. Add the wine to the pan and stir to dissolve any drippings. Scrape the bones and liquid into a medium saucepan. Add the broth and bay leaves. Bring the broth to a simmer. Stir in the vegetables. Cover and simmer for 60 minutes. Strain the broth, return it to the saucepan, and reduce it over medium heat to 2 cups/500 mL. Reserve.

Shortly before serving, reheat the jus. Season it with salt and pepper, and stir in the sage leaves just to heat through. Serve immediately.

The sage is added at the end to preserve its fragrance.

Roast Garlic–Stuffed Squab

Preheat the oven to 400°F/200°C.

Roast the whole garlic heads in a small pan until they begin to bubble through the top, about 60 minutes. Let cool to room temperature. Using a serrated knife, trim off just enough of the top to expose the cloves. Squeeze the roasted garlic out carefully and discard any stray skin pieces.

Preheat the oven to 350°F/180°C.

In a medium skillet over medium heat, cook the bacon until it is crisp. Add the shallots and chicken livers and sauté, stirring frequently, just until the livers are cooked through and lightly caramelized. Add the wine and continue cooking, stirring occasionally, as it reduces and glazes the livers. Scrape the pan contents into a food processor. Add the bread crumbs and garlic. Process until well combined. Season with salt and pepper.

Stuff the squabs with the mixture. Pat the birds into an even round shape. Pull the legs together on the end of the squab and tie them together with a paper twist tie or butcher string. The birds may be prepared to this point the day before and refrigerated. If so let them rest at room temperature for 30 minutes before cooking. Set the birds in a small roasting pan and roast for 30 to 40 minutes, until a meat thermometer inserted in a fleshy part of the bird registers 145°F/65°C. Let rest, covered with foil, for 5 minutes. Cut the squab in half through the center, then slice each half into 3 pieces for fanning out on the plate.

Meat thermometers are an excellent way to judge the doneness of an ingredient. The pros can judge doneness by instinct and touch, but as you're climbing that ladder a thermometer is a good aid.

2 heads garlic

4 slices bacon

2 large shallots, minced

1 cup / 250 mL chicken livers

1 cup / 250 mL Cabernet Sauvignon

1 cup / 250 mL fresh bread crumbs

Salt and pepper to taste

Reserved semi-boneless squab

Ground-Cherry Chutney

¼ cup / 60 mL sugar

2 tablespoons / 25 mL water

½ cup / 125 mL minced onion

¼ cup / 60 mL white wine vinegar

1 cup / 250 mL ground-cherries*

Salt and pepper to taste

*GROUND-CHERRIES ARE AVAILABLE IN THE
SUMMER AND FALL FROM FARMERS' MARKETS IN
NORTH AMERICA OR FROM NEW ZEALAND,
WHERE THEY ARE CALLED PHYSALIS. GOOSE-
BERRIES MAY BE USED OR EVEN REGULAR
CHERRIES.

In a small, heavy saucepan over low heat, melt the sugar and water, swirling gently just to dissolve it. Increase the heat to medium-low and simmer the syrup until it begins to caramelize. Swirl the pan gently to prevent burning. When the caramel is light brown, add the onions and vinegar (the caramel will bubble up). Bring the mixture to a simmer, stirring frequently, until it thickens. Add the cherries and just heat the mixture through. Season with salt and pepper. Reserve.

Wild Rice Almond Pudding

1 cup / 250 mL wild rice

3 cups / 750 mL water

2 heads garlic

Soft butter

½ cup / 125 mL sliced almonds, toasted and chopped

2 eggs

½ cup / 125 mL heavy cream

Salt and pepper to taste

Preheat the oven to 400°F/200°C.

Place the rice and water in a medium saucepan and simmer, covered, until the rice absorbs the water and softens, revealing its inside kernel, 45 to 60 minutes. Add a bit more water if needed to finish cooking. When the rice is cooked through, briefly stir it over high heat to dry it.

Meanwhile, roast the whole garlic heads in a small pan until they begin to bubble through the top, about 60 minutes. Let cool to room temperature. Using a serrated knife, trim off just enough of the top to expose the cloves. Squeeze the contents out carefully and discard any stray skin pieces.

Preheat the oven to 350°F/180°C.

Brush 4 (¾-cup/175 mL) ramekins with the soft butter and coat them thoroughly with the toasted almonds. (Pour all of the almonds into 1 ramekin and hold it over a second ramekin as you turn it to coat the inside. Pour the remaining almonds into the second ramekin and repeat the procedure.)

Place half of the rice in a food processor. Add the eggs, cream, and the garlic and process until smooth. Add the remaining rice, season with salt and pepper, and pulse just to stir. Divide the mixture between the ramekins and set them in a roasting pan. Pour simmering water into the pan to come halfway up the sides of the ramekins. Bake the puddings for 30 to 40 minutes until set in the middle. Let rest briefly before serving.

The water bath insulates the delicate pudding from the direct heat of the oven that would cause the eggs to puff then collapse, squeezing moisture out of the pudding.

The Plate!

Quickly invert a wild rice pudding onto each of 4 plates. Fan the squab slices around it. Ladle some jus over the slices. Top with some chutney and a sage sprig. Serve with a flutter!

Sage sprigs

◈ WILD RICE ◈

Wild rice is neither a rice nor wild. This unique grain, native to North America, is cultivated extensively in the Great Lakes region. Its distinctive nutty wine-like flavors are a favorite of chefs, who prize those varieties whose grains are the longest. Harvesting it is difficult, as it grows only in bogs and must be treated delicately — hence its often forbidding price.

Brown Butter Blueberry Cashew Tart
with Crusted Caramel Ice Cream,
Pink Peppercorn Sauce, and Caramel Cashew Brittle

By now you've probably noticed that I like to brown things. Well, butter is no different.
Brown butter and blueberries escort sophisticated pink peppercorn to a dessert land where
leftovers are unheard of. I know, I've been there!

◈ 4 SERVINGS, WITH LEFTOVERS ◈

TIMING: MAKE THE ICE CREAM BASE THE DAY BEFORE. | MAKE THE ICE CREAM AND FREEZE IT SEVERAL HOURS OR THE DAY BEFORE.
THE TART MAY ALSO BE MADE THE DAY BEFORE. | MAKE THE BRITTLE AND SAUCE WHILE THE TART BAKES.

Crusted Caramel Ice Cream

1 cup / 250 mL sugar

½ cup / 125 mL water

2 cups / 500 mL heavy cream

2 cups / 500 mL milk

4 egg yolks

1 tablespoon / 15 mL vanilla

½ teaspoon / 2 mL salt

Caramel cashew brittle (page 159)

In a medium, heavy saucepan over low heat, melt the sugar and water, swirling gently just to dissolve it. Increase the heat to high and boil the syrup, gently swirling the caramel as it begins to color.

When it reaches an even deep golden brown, add the cream and milk (the caramel will bubble up). Bring the mixture to a simmer, stirring to dissolve the caramel.

In a medium bowl, whisk together the egg yolks, vanilla, and salt. Whisking constantly, slowly add the hot caramel. Return the mixture to the pot and heat over medium-low heat, stirring constantly, until it is thick enough to coat the back of a spoon.

Strain the custard through a fine-mesh strainer and chill it quickly by placing it in the freezer or in an ice bath for 15 minutes.

Freeze the custard in an ice-cream maker following the manufacturer's instructions. Transfer the ice cream to an airtight container and freeze it until hard.

Shortly before serving, grind one-quarter of the brittle to a powder in a food processor. Spread the powder in a shallow dish. Using an ice-cream scoop, form balls of the ice cream. Roll them in the caramel powder and serve immediately.

When ice cream is first made it's not much cooler than the freezing point of water. Its softness at that point is quite appealing — try it! Freeze it longer if you prefer it harder.

Cashew Tart Crust

In a food processor, process the cashews, flour, and sugar until they are thoroughly combined and the nuts are finely chopped. Add the frozen butter and process until the mixture resembles coarse crumbs. Add the egg yolk and process just to combine.

Lightly flour your hands. Remove the dough and pat it into a ball. Wrap it in plastic wrap and refrigerate it for at least 30 minutes.

Preheat the oven to 400°F/200°C.

On a lightly floured work surface, roll out the dough ¼-inch/5 mm thick. Fit it into a 10 by 1-inch/25 by 2.5 cm tart mold with removable bottom or several smaller tart molds. Prick the shell evenly with a fork and line the shell with parchment paper weighted down with a layer of dried beans. Bake the tart shell until it is a light golden brown, 10 to 15 minutes. Let cool on a rack.

Much of the strength of this crust is derived from the nuts. If they are coarse and chunky, they are weaker. The object of prebaking is to set the crust before the moist filling weakens it. It will bake further, so don't allow it to get too brown at this stage.

1 cup / 250 mL cashews

¾ cup / 175 mL all-purpose flour

⅓ cup / 75 mL sugar

¼ pound / 125 g frozen butter (½ cup / 125 mL), chopped

1 egg yolk

Brown Butter Blueberry Filling

¾ cup / 175 mL butter, cut into pieces

1 vanilla bean (or 1 teaspoon / 5 mL vanilla)

3 eggs

1 cup / 250 mL sugar

½ cup / 125 mL all-purpose flour

3 cups / 750 mL blueberries

Preheat the oven to 350°F/180°C.

In a medium saucepan, melt the butter over high heat. The foam will subside, then a second foam will begin to rise. At this point watch it carefully and swirl it gently. When the milk-fat solids in the bottom are a rich brown and the butter has a very pleasing nutty smell, remove it from the heat and pour it into a heatproof bowl to stop the cooking.

Cut the vanilla bean lengthwise and scrape the seeds into a medium bowl. Add the eggs, sugar, and flour and whisk until blended. Add the brown butter and whisk it into the mix completely.

Fill the tart shell almost completely with the berries, then pour the batter evenly over them. Bake the tart until set, 30 to 45 minutes depending on its size.

Cool the tart on a rack to room temperature and serve or refrigerate and bring back to room temperature before serving.

Until you master butter browning, keep an eye on the milk-fat solids under the foam — they can burn quickly and are the key to the butter's flavor. The object is to rid the butter of its 20 percent or so water and allow the remaining fat to rise gently in temperature until it toasts the particles. Until the water in the butter is gone, the overall temperature can't rise above the boiling point of the water to the higher temperatures needed for browning.

Caramel Cashew Brittle

Lightly oil a marble slab or other work surface (not wood).

In a large, heavy saucepan over high heat, melt the sugar, corn syrup, and water, stirring gently.

When a candy thermometer reaches 265°F/130°C, stir in the nuts. Continue cooking several minutes longer, stirring frequently, until the mixture reaches 310°F/155°C. Add the butter and vanilla and stir to thoroughly incorporate. Quickly stir in the baking soda.

Pour the mixture onto the marble slab. Put on heavy gloves and with a spatula first loosen it from the surface, then stretch it. Let it cool for 60 minutes.

Break the brittle into smaller pieces. Store them in an airtight container in a cool place.

The baking soda reacts with the heat of the candy and creates an intricate network of tiny bubbles that weakens the cooling candy, making it brittle, hence the name. I learned the hard way not to let the candy cool untouched on the work surface. It can stick like cement!

2 cups / 500 mL sugar

1 cup / 250 mL light corn syrup

1 cup / 250 mL water

2 cups / 500 mL cashews

2 tablespoons / 25 mL butter

1 teaspoon / 5 mL vanilla

1 teaspoon / 5 mL baking soda

Pink Peppercorn Sauce

6 egg yolks

½ cup / 125 mL sugar

2 tablespoons / 25 mL grenadine

1 teaspoon / 5 mL vanilla

1 cup / 250 mL milk

1 cup / 250 mL heavy cream

2 tablespoons / 25 mL pink peppercorns, crushed

In a medium bowl, whisk together the yolks, sugar, grenadine, and vanilla. In a medium saucepan over medium heat, bring the milk, cream, and peppercorns to a simmer. Stirring constantly, slowly pour the hot mixture into the yolk mixture. Return the mixture to the pot and heat it over medium-low heat, stirring constantly, until it is thick enough to coat the back of a spoon. Refrigerate the sauce until needed.

The Plate!

Wedges of cashew brittle

Spoon about ¼ cup/60 mL of the sauce onto each of 4 chilled plates. Add a slice of tart. Top it with a scoop of crusted ice cream. Garnish with a brittle wedge. Serve with a crunch!

> ### ❖ PEPPERCORNS ❖
>
> *Peppercorns are the berry of the Piper nigrum plant. Both green and black peppercorns are picked unripe; the greens are pickled, while the black peppercorns are allowed to dry in the sun. White peppercorns are left to ripen on the plant, ferment, and then have their skin removed, leaving them with a relatively mild flavor. Pink peppercorns are unrelated to other peppercorns. They are the dried berry of a South American rose plant, which accounts for their perfume-like flavor.*

Butterscotch-Glazed Apples and Yogurt Cheese in a Crisp Leaf with an Apple Fritter and Calvados Cider Sauce

Very often a chef will spot a technique in one recipe and adapt it for another. The cooking method for these apples was inspired by the treatment received by apples in the classic tarte Tatin. Anything simmered in butterscotch works for me!

◇ 6 SERVINGS ◇

TIMING: MAKE THE YOGURT CHEESE AND COOKIE BATTER THE DAY BEFORE.
| MAKE THE APPLES. | MAKE THE SAUCE. | FRY THE FRITTERS AT THE LAST SECOND.

Yogurt Cheese

Whisk the ingredients together until smooth. Place several layers of cheesecloth in a bowl. Pour in the yogurt. Gather the edges of the cheesecloth and fashion a bag.

Secure the bag with some string and hang the bag over the bowl for several hours in the refrigerator. The longer it hangs, the thicker the cheese will be; overnight it will become almost solid. Well over half of the yogurt will drain out in the form of liquid whey, which may be used as a drink.

Transfer the cheese to an airtight container and reserve it for 3 to 5 days, refrigerated, until needed.

2 cups / 500 mL yogurt

4 tablespoons / 60 mL light honey

1 teaspoon / 5 mL vanilla

Don't use non-fat yogurt varieties — they won't work in this method. The liquid whey that drains out is often used as a beverage or even to cook with in many cuisines.

Crisp Leaf Cookies

4 tablespoons / 60 mL butter

2 tablespoons / 25 mL honey

3 ounces / 75 g all-purpose flour

2 ounces / 50 g sugar

1 egg white

1 teaspoon / 5 mL cinnamon

1 teaspoon / 5 mL molasses

In a food processor, process the butter, honey, flour, sugar, and egg white together until they are very smooth and completely combined.

Refrigerate the batter in an airtight container until chilled. It may also be made the day before.

Preheat the oven to 350°F/180°C. Lightly oil a nonstick baking sheet or line it with a silicone baking mat or parchment paper.

Cut a 5-inch/12 cm stylized leaf template out of food-safe stiff plastic, leaving a border of several inches around the cut-out.

Place the template on the baking sheet and spread about 2 tablespoons/25 mL of the batter through it, smoothing with a metal spatula. Form at least 6 leaves, leaving 1 inch/2.5 cm between each.

Stir the cinnamon and molasses into the remaining batter and place it in a piping bag with a small plain tip. Pipe an outline of the darker batter along the edge of each leaf, and pipe "veins" onto each leaf.

Bake the leaves until crisp and lightly browned, about 10 minutes.

While the cookies are still hot, invert them onto crumpled foil to form a wind-blown shape. If the cookies harden, return them to the oven for a few seconds. Let them cool. Store in an airtight container for up to 1 day.

Try to form the leaves so that much of the back of the leaf is raised in the air, leaving a basket at its base for the weight of the anchoring apples.

Butterscotch-Glazed Apples

Peel the apples. Using a large melon-ball cutter, cut out as many balls from the apples as possible.

In a small saucepan over medium-low heat, melt the sugar and water together, stirring to dissolve the sugar. Allow the syrup to boil, gently swirling it as it begins to brown. When it is an even deep golden brown, add the butter and stir to combine. Add the apple balls and reduce the heat to medium-low.

Simmer the balls, without stirring, for 30 to 45 minutes as they release their juices and absorb the butterscotch. Let rest or serve immediately.

Don't stir the apples once they begin to soften, or they will mash and lose their shape. Observe the syrup's thickness: it will evolve from thin to thick to thin and back again before the apples have finished releasing their moisture and can begin absorbing the butterscotch.

6 apples

1 cup / 250 mL sugar

½ cup / 125 mL water

¼ pound / 125 g butter (½ cup / 125 mL)

Calvados Cider Sauce

Place the apple in a small saucepan with the cider and butter. Bring the mixture to a simmer and cook until the apples become mushy. Add the brandy and simmer a few moments more.

Purée the mixture in a blender until smooth. Strain it through a fine-mesh strainer. Season with salt. Refrigerate until needed.

Taste the cider first. If it's not strongly flavored, reduce more to make enough for the sauce. I like using distinct heirloom apple varieties such as the Macoun or McIntosh to flavor this sauce.

2 apples, unpeeled, cored, and chopped

1 cup / 250 mL apple cider

4 tablespoons / 60 mL butter

¼ cup / 60 mL Calvados

Salt to taste

Apple Fritters

1 cup / 250 mL apple cider

1 tablespoon / 15 mL cornstarch

1 teaspoon / 5 mL baking powder

1 cup / 250 mL all-purpose flour

½ cup / 125 mL sugar

1 tablespoon / 15 mL cinnamon

4 cups / 1 L vegetable oil

6 apple rings, ½-inch / 1 cm thick, cores removed (from about 2 apples)

In a medium bowl, stir together the cider, cornstarch, and baking powder. Stir in enough of the flour to form a stiff batter.

In another bowl, stir together the sugar and cinnamon.

In a high-sided pan, heat the oil until it reaches 365°F/185°C. Dip the apple rings in the batter and drop them carefully into the oil. Fry in batches if necessary. Turn the fritters so they brown on all sides. (The fritters may also be fried in a countertop deep-fryer, following the manufacturer's instructions.) When the fritters are golden brown, remove them with a slotted spoon and drain them on paper towels. Toss the fritters in the sugar mixture and serve immediately.

The fritters are great all by themselves as a special treat. If the batter is too thick, add a bit of water; if it's too thin, slowly whisk in flour.

The Plate!

Pour about ¼ cup/60 mL of the sauce onto each of 6 plates. Position a fritter in the center of the plate and top it with an apple leaf. Fill the leaf with apple balls and top with the yogurt cheese. Serve with a mmm!

◈ APPLES ◈

One of my earliest food memories is of exploring the apple orchards around my home in the Hudson Valley of New York. My brothers and I would climb the trees and gorge ourselves with any number of varieties. At the time we had no idea what a Granny Smith apple was. We sure knew what a Mother Smith apple pie tasted like, though. To this day I look forward to going home for several slices of my mom's famous pie!

Strawberry Mint Compote
in a Crisp Cookie Cup with
Strawberry Wine Ice and Lemonade Sauce

Awesome ingredients like just-picked, warm-from-the-sun, and perfectly ripe strawberries inspire plates like this. As elaborate as this dessert may seem, it relies on the amazing flavor of fresh local berries for perfection. Don't waste the effort on poor hard, well-traveled half-berries.

◇ 4 SERVINGS, WITH LEFTOVERS ◇

TIMING: MAKE THE WINE ICE AND THE COOKIE CUP BATTER THE DAY BEFORE. | MAKE THE LEMONADE SAUCE AND COOKIES. | MAKE THE COMPOTE.

Strawberry Wine Ice

Pour about 1 cup of the wine into a medium saucepan and add the sugar. Heat over medium heat, stirring gently, just long enough to melt the sugar. Stir in the remaining wine and remove from the heat.

Pour the mixture into a shallow pan. Cover it, and freeze it overnight.

1 bottle strawberry wine

1 ½ cups / 375 mL sugar

Since sugar and alcohol can't freeze, this ice won't become rock hard as water would.

Crisp Cookie Cups

Place the corn syrup, sugar, and butter in a small saucepan over medium heat. Stir until the butter melts and the ingredients are combined. Add the flour, remove from the heat, and stir until a smooth batter is formed. Refrigerate the batter overnight.

Preheat the oven to 350°F/180°C. Lightly oil a baking sheet.

Form balls with 1 tablespoon/15 mL of the chilled cookie batter. Place the balls 4 inches apart on the baking sheet. Bake until the batter spreads out and turns a deep golden brown, about 10 minutes.

⅓ cup / 75 mL corn syrup

⅓ cup / 75 mL sugar

4 tablespoons / 60 mL butter

½ cup / 125 mL all-purpose flour

continued >>

Let the cookies cool for a few minutes until they become pliable. Working quickly, invert each cookie onto a small cup or other form and press the sides of the cookie down to form a cup shape. If the cookies have cooled too much, they will be harder to form without breaking; return them to the oven briefly if necessary. Let the cookie cups cool completely, and remove them from the forms. Store the cookie cups in an airtight container until ready for use.

Chilling the batter makes it easier to work with, but it will still bake easily when warm. Don't make the balls too big: they will spread dramatically. Make sure that the cookies are evenly browned before removing them from the oven. If the cookies brown unevenly in your oven, remove the ones that are ready and form them. Bake the remaining cookies until golden brown. The lighter the color, the weaker the cookie cup and the more likely it will be to stick to your teeth as you eat it. The upper surface of these cookies is more textured than the bottom; flipping the cookie onto the form shows off the texture.

Lemonade Sauce

Zest and juice of 6 lemons

3 Granny Smith apples, peeled, cored, and chopped (about 4 cups / 1 L)

2 cups / 500 mL water

½ cup / 125 mL sugar

¼ teaspoon / 1 mL salt

Combine the lemon juice and zest, apple, water, sugar, and salt in a saucepan, and bring the mixture to a simmer. Cover, and continue simmering until the apples are soft, about 10 minutes.

Pour the lemon mixture into a blender and purée it until very smooth. Strain it through a fine-mesh strainer. Pour the purée into a storage container, and refrigerate until chilled, at least 2 hours.

Granny Smith apples will not oxidize and turn brown, discoloring the sauce. The fragrant lemon flavor of the sauce is entirely dependent on the lemon zest. Taste the sauce before you add the salt. You'll see that salt is just as important for sweet preparations as it is for savory ones.

Strawberry Mint Compote

Toss all the ingredients together until well combined. Let them rest for a few minutes before serving.

1 pint / 500 mL ripe strawberries

2 to 3 tablespoons / 25 to 45 mL light honey

2 tablespoons / 25 mL finely sliced mint

The Plate!

Pour ¼ cup/60 mL of the lemonade sauce in the center of each of 4 chilled plates. Place a cookie cup in the center of each plate. Fill the cup with some of the berry compote. Spoon some of the wine ice on top. Garnish with a mint sprig. Serve with a brrr!

Mint sprigs

❖ STRAWBERRIES ❖

"Wee can not sett downe foote but tred on strawberries," wrote the first Englishman to encounter this prized fruit in the New World. At that time it was only possible to eat them where they grew, but today food scientists, in their infinite wisdom, have created cartoon strawberries that can travel great distances. Unfortunately they retain none of the wonderful fragrant ripeness of a warm-from-the-sun ripe berry. Progress? For the real thing, and a definitive summer experience, find a local grower and pick them yourself!

Oatmeal Crisp Raspberry and Saffron Lemon Curd Napoleon with Raspberry Leather, Riesling Sauce, and Caramel Raspberries

In my world, it's hard not to think about taste and flavor combinations, sometimes in places other than the kitchen. I was wave sailing when I decided to try out saffron and raspberries. What a breeze I was having that day!

◇ 6 SERVINGS ◇

TIMING: MAKE THE RASPBERRY LEATHER, COOKIE BATTER, LEMON CURD, AND ZEST THE DAY BEFORE. | MAKE THE RIESLING SAUCE AND RASPBERRY SQUEEZE UP TO 1 DAY AHEAD. | MAKE THE CARAMEL RASPBERRIES ABOUT 1 HOUR AHEAD. | AT THE LAST SECOND, ASSEMBLE THE NAPOLEONS.

Raspberry Leather

2 cups / 500 mL peeled and chopped green apples (about 1 ½ apples)

2 cups / 500 mL fresh or frozen raspberries

1 cup / 250 mL sugar

¼ cup / 60 mL framboise liqueur

Preheat the oven to 150°F/65°C. Line a baking sheet with a silicone baking mat or a lightly oiled piece of waxed paper.

Place all the ingredients in a medium saucepan and bring to a simmer. Simmer for about 5 minutes, until the apples become mushy.

In a blender, purée the mixture until very smooth. Pour it onto the silicone mat. Dry the leather in the oven at least 4 hours or even overnight. (The leather can also be dried in a convection oven at 200°F/95°C for 20 minutes. Better yet, dehydrate it in a home food dehydrator.) When it is finished drying, the leather will be strong and flexible.

Let the leather cool on the baking sheet. As it cools, peel the dried fruit off the mat and rest it on a sheet of wax paper. When it is completely cooled, roll the fruit up and store until needed.

Cut the fruit into 18 slivers 4 inches/10 cm long.

Raspberries don't have enough pectin to strengthen into leather, so they need the boost of the apples' pectin.

Oatmeal Crisps

Place the oats, sugar, flour, cornstarch, and baking powder in a food processor and pulse just to mix, leaving the oats somewhat coarse. Add the melted butter and egg and mix just long enough to combine.

Let the batter cool briefly and use it immediately, or refrigerate it. It may also be made ahead to this point.

Preheat the oven to 375°F/190°C. Lightly oil a baking sheet.

Cut a 3-inch/8 cm circle out of a stiff piece of food-safe plastic, leaving a border of several inches.

Place the template on the baking sheet and spread 1 tablespoon/15 mL of the batter through it, using a small metal spatula to make an even, thin layer. Repeat with the remaining batter. You will need 3 crisps for each napoleon and a few extras.

Bake until the batter becomes crisp and golden brown.

Loosen the crisps from the baking surface as they cool, and cool completely on a rack. Store in an airtight container.

Reserve several tablespoons of the unground oats and stir them in at the end for a rustic look. The baking soda raises the baking batter slightly with a network of tiny bubbles. When it finishes baking, that intricate structure crisps and becomes crunchy.

1 cup / 250 mL large-flake oats

1 cup / 250 mL sugar

1 tablespoon / 15 mL all-purpose flour

1 tablespoon / 15 mL cornstarch

1 teaspoon / 5 mL baking powder

¼ pound / 125 g butter (½ cup / 125 mL), melted

1 egg

Saffron Lemon Curd

Juice of 4 lemons, zest reserved

¼ pound / 125 g butter (½ cup / 125 mL)

1 cup / 250 mL sugar

½ teaspoon / 2 mL saffron threads

4 eggs

In the top of a double boiler over simmering water, gently heat the lemon juice, butter, sugar, and saffron, stirring until well blended. Let rest a few minutes as the saffron steeps.

Whisk in the eggs and stir until thickened. Refrigerate the curd, covered, until chilled.

The saffron needs a few minutes of steeping to fully develop its flavors. This method of making curd is essentially a controlled curdling of the egg yolks, hence the name.

Candied Lemon Zest

½ cup / 125 mL water

½ cup / 125 mL sugar

Reserved lemon zest

Heat the water and sugar gently in a small saucepan, stirring until the sugar is dissolved. Add the zest and simmer for a few minutes, just to heat it through. Remove from the heat and let cool.

Preheat the oven to 250°F/120°C.

Remove the zest and place it on a lightly oiled baking sheet. Dry in the oven for 15 minutes or so, until crisp. Reserve in an airtight container.

An older method still common is to cut, with a small knife or vegetable peeler, thin strips of the skin that includes the pith beneath, and then repeat the syrup making several times, simmering the peel in successive fresh batches until its bitterness dissipates and with it the lemon fragrance. Modern cooking stresses flavor retention.

Riesling Sauce

Combine the apples, honey, and 1 ½ cups/375 mL of the wine in a small saucepan. Bring them to a simmer, and simmer until the apples become mushy, about 10 minutes.

Pour the apples into a blender and add the remaining wine. Purée the sauce until smooth. Strain it through a fine-mesh strainer and season with the salt. Refrigerate it until needed.

3 Granny Smith apples, peeled, cored, and chopped (about 4 cups / 1 L)

½ cup / 125 mL honey

3 cups / 750 mL Riesling (preferably late harvest)

¼ teaspoon / 1 mL salt

Raspberry Squeeze

Heat the ingredients together in a saucepan until the raspberries are mushy, about 5 minutes. Purée the mixture in a blender. Strain it through a fine-mesh strainer to remove the pips. Pour it into a squeeze bottle and refrigerate until needed.

1 cup / 250 mL fresh or frozen raspberries

1 cup / 250 mL any liquid, including water (try a red wine)

½ cup / 125 mL sugar

Caramel Raspberries

Half-fill a large saucepan with water. Lightly oil a baking sheet.

Melt the sugar, corn syrup, and water together in a medium saucepan over high heat, stirring to dissolve the sugar. Continue heating the syrup until a candy thermometer reads 320°F/160°C and the syrup just begins to darken slightly. Immediately place the smaller pot in the large pot of water to stop the cooking.

Let the caramel cool for a few minutes until it thickly coats a raspberry dipped in it. Poke a toothpick into a raspberry and roll the raspberry in the caramel. Place it

2 cups / 500 mL sugar

1 cup / 250 mL corn syrup

1 cup / 250 mL water

24 raspberries

continued >>

on the baking sheet. Repeat with the remaining raspberries and allow to cool. Reserve for up to several hours.

The corn syrup has a different molecular structure from sugar and helps keep the sugar syrup from crystallizing, which would ruin the caramel.

The Napoleons

Several cups fresh raspberries

Place a spoonful of the curd on each of 2 oat crisps and spread it out evenly. Add a layer of raspberries nestled together. Place 1 disk on the other and cap with a third crisp. Voilà: a napoleon! Repeat the procedure to make 5 more napoleons.

The Plate!

Pour about ¼ cup/60 mL of the Riesling sauce onto each of 6 chilled plates. Gently place a napoleon in the center of the sauce. Drape 3 slivers of fruit leather from the center of the top crisp down the side of the napoleon and into the sauce. Decorate the plate with some raspberry squeeze, and top each napoleon with a caramel raspberry. Sprinkle with some candied zest. Add 3 more caramel raspberries around the plate. Serve with a sweet tooth!

◈ SAFFRON ◈

Saffron is prized for its distinctive perfume and luminous color. It is the dried stigma of a specific crocus plant native to the Mediterranean. Its high price reflects the fact that there are only three stigmas per plant and they must be harvested by hand. It takes well over 100,000 plants to yield a scant pound of the spice — fortunately a little goes a long way!

A Time for Chocolate: Chocolate Coconut Clock Tower with Cookie Clock Hands, Roast Pineapple Vanilla Sauce, and the Correct Time

Every chef worth his salt prides himself on his chocolate presentation skills.
I always start out with more chocolate than I need, to account for its mysterious shrinkage as I create
with it, surrounded by sharp-eyed cooks. Works every time!

◈ 8 SERVINGS ◈

TIMING: MAKE THE MOUSSE THE DAY BEFORE. | WHILE THE MOUSSE CHILLS, MAKE THE BROWNIES. WRAP THEM WITH THE
CHOCOLATE COLLARS AND CHILL TO SET. FILL WITH MOUSSE AND FREEZE OVERNIGHT.
| MAKE THE SAUCE AND THE COOKIE HANDS A FEW HOURS BEFORE.

Coconut Mousse

Place the chocolate, butter, liqueur, and coconut cream in a large stainless steel bowl. Place the bowl over a pot of gently simmering water. Melt the chocolate slowly, stirring frequently. As the chocolate melts, remove the bowl from the heat, returning briefly if needed. Stir until the mixture is very smooth and has cooled to room temperature.

In a separate bowl, whip the cream until it is stiff. Fold the cream into the chocolate until it is completely incorporated. Refrigerate the mousse until completely chilled, at least 2 hours.

12 ounces / 375 g white chocolate

¼ pound / 125 g butter (½ cup/ 125 mL)

4 tablespoons / 60 mL coconut liqueur

¼ cup / 60 mL coconut cream

½ cup / 125 mL heavy cream

In this method the white chocolate is needed to help stiffen the mousse as it cools; its blandness is hidden by the dominant coconut flavors. Don't overmix the whipped cream with the base or it will deflate. Fold it in with a rubber spatula.

Chocolate Clock Towers

THE BROWNIES:

4 ounces / 125 g unsweetened chocolate, coarsely chopped

¼ pound / 125 g butter (½ cup / 125 mL)

1 cup / 250 mL brown sugar

1 cup / 250 mL white sugar

1 tablespoon / 15 mL vanilla

4 eggs

1 cup / 250 mL all-purpose flour

1 cup / 250 mL macadamia nuts

THE CHOCOLATE WRAP:

2 ounces / 50 g white chocolate, chopped

8 ounces / 250 g bittersweet chocolate

8 ounces / 250 g milk chocolate

Reserved coconut mousse

1 cup / 250 mL toasted sweetened coconut, shredded

Make the brownie base: Preheat the oven to 350°F/180°C. Butter and flour a 9-inch/23 cm square baking pan.

Place the unsweetened chocolate, butter, brown sugar, white sugar, and vanilla in a medium bowl. Set the bowl over a pot of simmering water and stir until the mixture is melted and smooth. Remove it from the heat. Beat in the eggs. Beat in the flour. Stir in the nuts. Pour the batter into the baking pan and bake for 30 minutes or until a toothpick inserted in the cake comes out clean. Let the brownies cool, then cut out 8 circles using a 3-inch/8 cm biscuit cutter. Pass around the scraps on a plate.

Make the chocolate wrap: Cut 8 pieces of parchment or wax paper measuring 11 by 3 inches/25 by 8 cm.

Melt the white chocolate in a bowl set over a simmering pot of water, stirring until smooth. Place the melted chocolate in a small piping bag fitted with a very small plain tip. Pipe the chocolate in an even lattice or other fanciful pattern onto the papers. Place them in a cool place to set.

Temper the bittersweet chocolate and milk chocolates separately. (Tempering the chocolate gives it a shiny glaze. You may skip this step. Simply melt the chocolate just as you melted the white chocolate and proceed to the next step.) Reserve one-third of the bittersweet chocolate in 1 or 2 large pieces. Chop the remaining two-thirds and place in a bowl. Set the bowl over a pot of simmering water. When the chocolate begins to melt, stir it until it is smooth. Remove from the heat, add the large piece, and stir. As it melts slowly it adjusts the temperature of the melted chocolate, tempering it. Repeat with the milk chocolate.

Pour some of each chocolate into the center of each chocolate wrap over the white pattern. Using a small offset spatula, gently spread the chocolate into an even layer slightly thicker than the white chocolate. If you spill over the edges, wipe away the excess. Let the papers rest for several minutes as the white chocolate warms slightly. Reserve some of the bittersweet chocolate in a small piping bag for the plate decoration.

Carefully, quickly, and accurately wrap the chocolate around a brownie round, wax paper facing out. Try to have it only slightly overlap, forming a perfect seam. Adjust the paper collars until they are even, straight, and tall. Transfer the contraptions to a baking sheet and refrigerate to set, 15 minutes.

Meanwhile, place the coconut mousse in a piping bag with a large plain tip. When the wraps are solid, quickly pipe the mousse evenly into each mold. Smooth the surface of each, making the top of the mousse perfectly flush with the chocolate collar. Sprinkle with the toasted coconut. Freeze until firm, 2 hours.

The white chocolate must be allowed to cool so it doesn't melt and remains distinct when the warmer dark chocolates are added. Properly tempering the chocolate gives it strength and sheen and makes it release easier from the paper. Pros use stiff thin plastic so the collars stand perfectly straight. Once the chocolate sets it is remarkably easy to peel off the collar lining.

Pineapple Vanilla Sauce

1 large, very ripe, fragrant pineapple, peeled, cored, and chopped

¼ pound / 125 g butter (½ cup / 125 mL), melted

½ cup / 125 mL brown sugar

3 cups / 750 mL pineapple juice

4 vanilla beans, pods split and seeds scraped out

Salt to taste

Preheat the oven to 400°F/200°C.

Toss the pineapple chunks with the butter and sugar. Place them in a roasting pan and roast for 15 minutes. Shake the pan. Continue roasting, shaking the pan or stirring the chunks every few minutes so they roast evenly, just until the pineapple is lightly caramelized, about another 15 minutes.

Transfer the pineapple to a medium saucepan. Pour the juice into the roasting pan and stir until any remaining bits have dissolved. Pour the juice into the saucepan. Add the vanilla bean pods and seeds. Bring the mixture to a gentle simmer. Simmer until the pineapple softens and begins to dissolve, about 30 minutes. Discard the vanilla pods. Purée the sauce in a blender until very smooth. Strain it through a fine-mesh strainer and chill until needed.

Keep an eye on the pineapple as it roasts so the drippings in the pan don't burn. If necessary splash some water in to keep the drippings dissolved. The simmering is needed to rehydrate and soften the toughened roast pineapple so it will purée easily.

Cookie Clock Hands

4 tablespoons / 60 mL butter, at room temperature

4 tablespoons / 60 mL molasses

⅔ cup / 150 mL sugar

⅔ cup / 150 mL all-purpose flour

3 egg whites

Place the butter, molasses, and sugar in a food processor and process until very smooth. Add the flour and egg whites and continue processing until thoroughly combined and smooth. Refrigerate the batter until firm, at least 2 hours.

Preheat the oven to 350°F/180°C.

Using a piece of thin, stiff food-safe plastic, cut out 2 clock hand templates, one 5 inches/12 cm long and the other 3 inches/8 cm long, and both at least ½ inch/1 cm wide for strength. Place the templates on a nonstick baking sheet.

Using a small metal spatula, spread a thin layer of the batter through the template. Repeat until 8 long hands and 8 short hands have been formed. Bake them until they are crisp and brown, 7 to 10 minutes. Let the cookie clock hands cool before gently removing them from the baking sheet. Reserve in an airtight container.

The Plate!

Remove the clock towers from the freezer. Grasp the small overlap area of the paper wrap and break it loose. Continue peeling the paper from the mold.

Using the reserved bittersweet chocolate, pipe a stylized clock face around the rim of 8 plates. Pour about ¼ cup/60 mL of the sauce in the center of each plate. Center a clock tower on the plate. Top with a truffle. Fit 2 clock hands in under the truffle to show the current time. Serve with a tick-tock!

8 chocolate truffles

◇ VANILLA ◇

Ever heard of hydroxy-4 methoxy-3 benzaldehyde? Artificial vanilla flavor is a triumph of food chemistry. Or is it? Real vanilla is derived from the seedpod of an orchid vine native to Central America. It is now grown throughout the tropics and must be hand fertilized, hand picked, and generally treated with such care that it becomes very expensive. That expense is well worth the true sensation of this fragrant complex flavor, which is quite unlike its unrelated scientific imitator.

Molten Dark Chocolate Cake
with Mocha Sauce, Cappuccino Froth, and
Orange Marmalade Mint Compote

To me this is chocolate fully realized, a warm cake oozing flavor. Of course I couldn't resist the urge to add some of my other favorite flavors. A crashing crescendo for the end of the meal!

◇ 6 SERVINGS ◇

TIMING: MAKE THE MARMALADE AND THE CAKE BATTER THE DAY BEFORE. | FINISH THE COMPOTE AND MAKE THE MOCHA SAUCE
A FEW HOURS BEFORE. JUST BEFORE SERVING, BAKE THE CAKES. | MAKE THE FROTH WHILE THE CAKES ARE BAKING.

Orange Marmalade Mint Compote

4 oranges

1 cup / 250 mL sugar

½ cup / 125 mL water

1 cup / 250 mL orange juice

½ cup / 125 mL Grand Marnier

½ cup / 125 mL chopped mint

Chop 2 of the oranges; remove all seeds and set aside. Place the sugar and water in a small, heavy saucepan and bring the mixture to a simmer, stirring gently until the sugar has dissolved. Simmer the syrup until it begins to darken around the edges. Gently swirl the pot as the caramel darkens. Be vigilant and be ready.

When the caramel is a deep golden brown, carefully add the chopped oranges and the orange juice, stopping the hot caramel from browning further. Bring the mixture to a simmer, stirring as the caramel dissolves and the mixture reduces. Simmer it for 30 minutes, stirring it frequently to prevent it from sticking or burning. The marmalade will thicken.

Remove the pan from the heat and stir in the Grand Marnier. Pour the mixture into a food processor and chop it coarsely. Let the marmalade cool, then refrigerate it overnight or for several weeks while the flavors blend.

Reserve ½ cup/125 mL of the marmalade in a bowl to finish the compote and serve the rest with your favorite toast.

Section the remaining 2 oranges: Carefully cut off their skins just to the flesh of the orange. Using a very sharp, small knife, cut down each side of the membranes and lift out the orange sections.

Squeeze the core, juicing it into the reserved marmalade. Stir in the chopped mint. Add the orange sections and stir them in carefully so they don't break. Let the compote rest for a few hours.

The key to marmalade is to mellow out the bitterness of the orange skins. The flavors are best after a week of rest in the refrigerator.

Molten Dark Chocolate Cake

Place the chocolate, butter, and allspice in a large stainless steel bowl. Place the bowl over a pot of simmering water. As the chocolate begins to melt, stir it until it is smooth. When about one-quarter of the unmelted chocolate remains, remove the bowl from the heat and continue stirring until all the chocolate is melted.

In a separate bowl, whisk together the egg yolks, sugar, molasses, and vanilla. Add the yolk mixture to the chocolate mixture and stir until combined. Add the flour and cocoa powder, and stir to combine.

In a separate bowl, whip the egg whites with a mixer on high speed until they stand in stiff peaks. Add one-third of the egg whites to the chocolate mixture and stir until completely combined. Using a rubber spatula, gently fold in the remaining egg whites until completely combined. Place the batter in a storage container and refrigerate until thoroughly chilled, about 2 hours, or up to 2 days.

Preheat the oven to 400°F/200°C. Lightly butter and flour 6 (¾-cup/ 175 mL) baking molds. Divide the chilled batter between the molds. Place the molds on a baking sheet and bake for exactly 12 minutes. Let the cakes stand for 2 minutes before serving.

8 ounces / 250 g bittersweet chocolate

¼ pound / 125 g butter (½ cup / 125 mL)

½ teaspoon / 2 mL ground allspice

5 eggs, separated

¼ cup / 60 mL sugar

2 tablespoons / 25 mL molasses

2 teaspoons / 10 mL vanilla

1 cup / 250 mL all-purpose flour

2 tablespoons / 25 mL cocoa powder

Mocha Sauce

½ cup / 125 mL milk

½ cup / 125 mL heavy cream

4 tablespoons / 60 mL sugar

2 tablespoons / 25 mL very finely ground coffee beans

4 ounces / 125 g bittersweet chocolate, chopped

Pinch of salt

In a small saucepan, bring the milk, cream, sugar, and coffee to a simmer, stirring. Remove it from the heat and let the mixture rest for a few minutes while the coffee flavor brews. Reheat it just to a simmer. Remove it from the heat and stir in the chocolate until it melts and the mixture becomes very smooth. Stir in the salt. Strain the sauce through a fine-mesh strainer.

Refrigerate the sauce.

Mocha refers to the flavor of chocolate and coffee together, a natural pairing. Try adjusting the ratio of the two ingredients to your taste for coffee.

Cappuccino Froth

2 egg yolks

2 tablespoons / 25 mL sugar

2 tablespoons / 25 mL milk

2 tablespoons / 25 mL Kahlua

Pinch of salt

Whisk together all of the ingredients in a stainless steel bowl. Place the bowl over a pot of simmering water.

Whisk the mixture constantly as the sauce aerates and then begins to thicken. This will take a few minutes of continuous whisking. Whisk until the sauce stands in soft peaks. Serve immediately.

This is the classic sabayon method. Don't over-whisk or the fragile sauce will break and collapse. If you're good, try making it over a direct flame like the pros.

The Plate!

Pour ¼ cup/60 mL of the cappuccino froth onto each of 6 plates. Add a few spoonfuls of the orange mint compote.

Unmold a molten chocolate cake and place it on the orange compote. Top the cake with a few spoonfuls of the mocha sauce. Using a vegetable peeler, peel a few shards of chocolate onto each plate. Top with a mint sprig. Serve with a twist!

Chocolate

Mint sprigs

◈ CHOCOLATE ◈

Chocolate is made from the seeds or beans of the cacao tree native to tropical America and now cultivated globally. The manufacturing process is long and complicated — one wonders whether divine intervention was responsible for its invention. Chocolate is hardened pure chocolate liquor. Its major components are cocoa powder and cocoa butter. Add sugar for bittersweet, add milkfat solids for milk chocolate, then remove the cocoa powder and white chocolate results. Avoid the versions that flood the market that are essentially chocolate-flavored palm kernel oil — the real thing is an epiphany.

The Menu Translated

◇

How often have you opened a restaurant menu only to be confronted with a deluge of chef-speak, of words and phrases that sound intimidating and confusing?

Maybe you have struggled to name a technique of your own devising and wish to be technically accurate in doing so. Or you may have wondered why everything that goes near a shallow pan seems to somehow become "sautéed"!

In an effort to bring some basic understanding to the often arcane language of cuisine, I have included the following plain-English definitions of some of the more commonly found culinary words. As with many attempts to define art forms, there can be a difference between the absolutely accurate and the practical definition of many of these terms. Next time you dine out, stroll into the kitchen and throw a few of these nuggets around — you'll either be "86ed" or offered a job!

Bake: A dry-heat cooking method that surrounds food with dry heated air in an enclosed space. It usually refers to the cooking of bread, pastries, and dessert dishes, although it sometimes may refer to fruit, vegetables, and fish. Generally identical to Roast, the main difference seems to be what's in the oven and the generally lower temperatures associated with baking.

Barbecue: To cook foods over a dry heat source such as a wood fire or gas or electric heat. The key word here is over as opposed to in or on the heat source. Generally, barbecue implies the use of a tangy and highly flavorful sauce that can be used as a marinade, a baste, or both. There are many regional variations on this method, all of which claim to be authentic and fortunately all are delicious. Essentially, Grill plus barbecue sauce!

Braise: My favorite cooking method, it involves first the surface searing of a generally tough and flavorful cut of meat followed by its long simmering until tender in a liquid that makes it more flavorful. Some cooks (criminals) skip the searing step and proceed directly to the simmering step, missing a flavor-building opportunity. It is sometimes used to describe a method where the food being braised, such as a tomato, is already tender or wouldn't benefit from the sear and really just cooks long enough to be flavored by a liquid more flavorful than itself. Got it?

Broil: A dry-heat cooking method that is defined by its heat source: above. If you manage to cook something with heat from above, it's broiled.

Broken: Generally refers to a mixture of two sauce-like elements that wouldn't normally combine, such as chive oil and Merlot reduction. The net effect is very positive and usually visually attractive.

Broth: A flavorful liquid that is made by simmering a variety of ingredients for a long time, extracting their flavors. To be accurate it must include meat, unlike Stock, which relies on bones.

Chiffonade: To slice very thinly. To be accurate it should refer only to leafy vegetables or herbs such as basil or spinach.

Compote: Today this term generally refers to any mixture of ingredients. However, classically it is a mixture of fruit cooked in a sugar syrup.

Coulis: A sauce that is most commonly based on a purée of fruit and less frequently vegetables. It may be hot or cold.

Crust: The outer layer of any type of food as long as it's crisp, hard, or crunchy.

Cure: Any method that involves drying, salting, smoking, or pickling and is designed to add flavor or storage life to a foodstuff.

Deglaze: To dissolve the flavorful particles remaining in a pan after something else has been cooked in it. This is generally accomplished by adding wine, stock, broth, or water to the pan and then using the resulting mixture as a flavor base for a sauce or glaze.

Demi-glace, Demi-glaze, or Demi: Technically a mixture of brown sauce and brown stock reduced to intensify its flavors. Today it generally — and often inaccurately — refers to any meat-based sauce, whether its flavors have been classically built or not.

Duxelle: Classically a mixture of mushrooms and onions sautéed in butter. Today it generally refers to anything that contains mushrooms and often omits the characteristic flavors of properly seared and caramelized mushrooms.

Emulsion: A mixture, often temporary and unstable, of two liquids that would not normally combine.

Flamed or Flambéed: Anything that has spent time in the presence of flaming liquor. A usually—but not always —beneficial process. You sometimes have to take the chef's word for it that there was ever any flame and further trust that the cook actually flamed if the chef wasn't looking.

Fry: A dry-heat cooking method that involves submerging the food in very hot and sometimes flavorful fat. Done properly it is a useful method for adding flavor and texture; screwed up it can result in fat-laden or burnt food.

Glaze: A thin, flavorful coating applied to the outside of a food item. It is generally achieved through the reduction and concentration of a liquid.

Gratin: A dish that is covered with cheese or bread crumbs and then browned. Very often the flavor-building browning step is omitted, lessening the potential of the dish.

Grill: To cook foods over a dry heat source such as a wood fire or gas or electric heat. Generally it implies the use of heated rods or bars that leave the characteristic cross-hatches of grilling.

Infuse: To flavor a food item through contact with another more flavorful food item.

Julienne: Anything that has been cut into a matchstick shape.

Jus: French for juice, this term is used to describe an accompanying sauce for a meat that features the juices, stock, or broth from that same meat. Generally the sauce is unthickened or barely thickened.

Macerate: To soak food in alcohol.

Marinate: To soak food in any flavorful liquid that is meant to flavor or even tenderize it.

Mélange: An overused term that seems to describe any mixture of ingredients.

Napoleon: Technically this term refers to a specific type of French layered pastry; in general use it refers to anything a chef can contrive to layer with something else.

Pavé: Technically this term refers to a layered cake. It is often appropriated to describe a layered vegetable presentation that is cut into individual pieces.

Pickled: Traditionally used to describe a preservation method, today this term refers to anything that has spent time in a flavored acidic liquid.

Poach: To cook something, fully submerged, in a gently simmering, very flavorful liquid.

Ragout: French for a stew that traditionally contained meat and vegetables. Today this term is loosely applied to any stew-like concoction regardless of its ingredients.

Reduction: A liquid that has simmered until its water has evaporated, thereby concentrating the flavors.

Roast: A dry-heat cooking method that surrounds food with dry heated air in an enclosed space. It usually refers to the cooking of meats and vegetables, although it sometimes may refer to fish. Generally identical to Bake, the main difference seems to be what's in the oven and the generally higher temperatures associated with roasting.

Sauce: Any flavorful liquid served with another food item. Generally it is thickened in some manner.

Sauté: Traditionally a cooking method that meant to "jump" something in hot fat. Today it seems to refer to anything that spends time in the ubiquitous sauté pan. Generally it's a high-heat quick method that employs the use of some type of fat.

Sear: To quickly brown the outside of a food item. It must be done over a high heat and is usually a prelude to another cooking method such as braising.

Smoke: Any cooking method that exposes the food to smoke of some kind. It traditionally was a preservation method but is now a flavoring method.

Steam: A moist-heat cooking method that exposes food to the high heat of steam.

Stock: A flavorful liquid that is made by simmering a variety of ingredients for a long time, extracting their flavors. To be accurate it must include bones, unlike Broth, which relies on meat scraps. It is sometimes also used to describe a purely vegetable-flavored liquid.

Sweat: To cook a food over a low heat until it begins to release its moisture. This term usually refers to vegetables.

Terrine: Traditionally a highly seasoned coarse meat dish baked in an earthenware terrine mold and served cold. Today the term includes anything prepared in a terrine mold and served cold.

Tian: A classic French term, similar to terrine, that describes a specific earthenware dish that food is prepared in. In this case it generally refers to a shallow square pan and has been adopted in a contemporary sense to refer to anything prepared in such a pan.

Index

About the Author

❖

Chef Michael Smith, C.E.C., has earned an international reputation for his contemporary creative cuisine.

A 1991 honors graduate of the Culinary Institute of America (New York), Michael has worked in elite kitchens in New York, London, Colorado, California, Texas, the Caribbean, and Venezuela. He has worked under David Bouley, Larry Forgione, Paul Sartory, and Albert Roux. In 1992, Michael took over as chef of The Inn at Bay Fortune on Prince Edward Island and turned it into a culinary destination. He is currently chef emeritus of the Inn and owns and operates Maple, a restaurant in Halifax, Nova Scotia.

In addition to hosting his own national TV cooking series, *The Inn Chef,* Michael has appeared on Burt Wolf's award-winning *A Taste For Travel,* Food Network's *In Food Today, Canada AM, Dini,* and *Canadian Living Television.* He has been written up in *The Globe and Mail, The National Post, The Toronto Star, The Montreal Gazette, Maclean's, Canadian Living, Chatelaine, Food & Wine, President's Choice Magazine, USA Today, The New York Times,* and *The Boston Globe.* Smith is also the author of *Open Kitchen: A Chef's Day at The Inn at Bay Fortune* (1998, Callawind Publications).

When he's not behind the stoves, Michael can be found windsurfing or mountain biking.

❖ CREDITS ❖

Front cover photo of Michael Smith and all black and white photography by Jack Leclair.

All color food photography by Julian Beverage.

Food styling by Craig Stelmack and Craig Conrad.

Food illustrations from the Artville Big Fruits and Vegetables collection.

Kitchen equipment courtesy of Paderno, KitchenAid, Rubbermaid, All-Clad, and Cuisipro.

Kitchen apparel courtesy of Chef Revival.